Donald F. Krill is an associate professor in the Graduate School of Social Work at the University of Denver and a private psychiatric social worker. His experience as a social worker includes positions with various medical facilities and extensive supervision of social work students. The author of numerous articles in professional social work journals, he also wrote the chapter entitled "Existential Social Work" for *Social Work Treatment*, edited by Francis J. Turner.

Existential Social Work

EXISTENTIAL SOCIAL WORK

Donald F. Krill

The Free Press
A Division of Macmillan Publishing Co., Inc.
NEW YORK

Collier Macmillan Publishers
LONDON

The Free Press
A Division of Macmillan Publishing Co., Inc.
866 Third Avenue, New York, N.Y. 10022

Collier Macmillan Canada, Ltd.

Library of Congress Catalog Card Number: 78-54132

Printed in the United States of America

printing number

1   2   3   4   5   6   7   8   9   10

Library of Congress Cataloging in Publication Data

Krill, Donald F
    Existential social work.

    (Treatment approaches in the human services)
    Bibliography: p.
    Includes index.
    1. Social service. 2. Existentialism. I. Title.
II. Series.
HV40.K7   361'.001   78-54132
ISBN 0-02-917830-4

In memory of my father,
Clarence William George Krill,
whose simplicity of living and humor
revealed what was needed.

Contents

Foreword

"Treatment Approaches in the Human Services" is the first series of professional texts to be prepared under the general auspices of social work. It is understandable that the editor and authors of this endeavor should be enthusiastic about its quality and prospects. But it is equally understandable that our enthusiasm is tempered with caution and prudence. There is a presumptuousness in attempting to be on the leading edge of thinking and aspiring to break new ground, and our professional experience urges us to be restrained.

The first suggestion for this series came from the editorial staff of The Free Press in the spring of 1975. At that time, the early responses to *Social Work Treatment** were available. It was clear from these responses that, useful as that book appeared to be, there was a wish and a need for more detail on each of the various thought systems covered, especially as regards their direct practice implications. These comments led to a proposal from the Free Press that a series be developed that would expand the content of the individual chapters of *Social Work Treatment* into full-length books with the objective of providing a richer and fuller exposition of each system. This idea is still germane to the series, but it has moved beyond the notion of expanding the chapters in the original collection with the emergence of new thought systems and theories. The amount of new thinking in the helping professions, the diversity of new demands, and the growing complexity of these demands have increased beyond the expectations of even the harbingers of the knowledge explosion of the early 1970s. No profession can or should stand still, and thus

---

*Francis J. Turner, ed., *Social Work Treatment,* Free Press, 1974.

no professional literature can be static. It is our hope that this series will stay continuously current as it takes account of new ideas emerging from practice.

By design, this series has a primary orientation to social work. But it is not designed for social workers alone; it is also intended to be useful to our colleagues in other professions. The point has frequently been made that much of the conceptual base of social work practice has been borrowed and that social work has made few original contributions to other professions. This is no longer true. A principal assumption of this series is that social work must now accept the responsibility for making available to other groups its rich accumulation of theoretical concepts and therapeutic strategies.

This responsibility to share does not presume that professions with a healing and human-development commitment are moving to some commonality of identity and structure. In the next decade, we are probably going to see clearer rather than more obscure professional identities, more precise professional boundaries, derived not from different knowledge bases but from differential use of shared knowledge. If this prediction is valid, it follows that each profession must develop increased and enriched ways of making available to other professions its own expanding knowledge of the human condition.

Although the books in this series are written from the viewpoint of of the clinician, they will be useful for the student-professional, the senior scholar, and the teacher of professionals as well. On the principle that no dynamic profession can tolerate division among its practitioners, theory builders, and teachers, each book is intended to be a bridging resource between practice and theory development. In directing this series to colleagues whose principal targets of practice are individuals, families, and groups, we take the other essential fields of practice as given. Thus the community-development, social action, policy, research, and service-delivery roles of the helping professions are not specifically addressed in these books.

One of the risks of living and practicing in an environment characterized by pluralism in professions, practice styles, and theoretical orientations is that one may easily become doctrinaire in defending a particular perspective. Useful and important as is ongoing debate that leads to clarification of similarities and differences, overlaps, and gaps in thought systems and theories, the authors of these books have been asked to minimize this function. That is, they are to analyze the conceptual base of their particular topic, identify its theoretical origins, explain and describe its operationalization in practice, but avoid polemics in behalf of "their" system. Inevitably, some material of this type is needed for comparisons, but the aim is to make the books explicative rather than argumentative.

Although the series has a clear focus and explicit objectives, there is also a strong commitment that it be marked with a quality of development and evolution. It is hoped that we will be responsive to changes in psychotherapeutic practice and to the needs of colleagues in practice and thus be ready to alter the format of subsequent books as may be necessary.

In a similar way, the ultimate number of books in the series has been left open. Viewing current practice in the late 1970s, it is possible to identify a large number of influential thought systems that need to be addressed. We can only presume that additional perspectives will emerge in the future. These will be addressed as the series continues, as will new developments or reformulations of existing practice perspectives.

The practice of psychotherapy and the wide spectrum of activities that it encompasses is a risky and uncertain endeavor. Clearly, we are just beginning a new era of human knowledge and improved clinical approaches and methods. At one time we were concerned because we knew so little; now we are concerned to use fully the rich progress that has been made in research, practice, and conceptualization. This series is dedicated to this task in the humble hope that it will contribute to man's concern for his fellows.

Donald Krill's book on existential social work practice is an important contribution to this series in that it represents a thorough analysis and presentation of a thought system of particular importance for therapeutic practice in the human services as it exists in this decade.

Although existential thinking has influenced many practitioners and theoreticians, especially since World War II, this influence has for the most part remained at a second level of abstraction (there are of course some notable exceptions to this such as Victor Frankl and Rollo May). That is, existential thinking has provided a philosophical basis for psychotherapeutic practice rather than a style of intervention in its own right. This has been particularly so in the existential literature in social work. As Krill mentions, there has been existentially oriented social work literature but little of it gave direction and assistance to the practitioner in applying existentialism to practice. This Donald Krill has done in a most helpful and imaginative way.

In addition to providing some direct and rich practice directions from this theoretical viewpoint, the author also addresses several other important questions. First, he raises the troubling yet essential question of the need for the therapist to be in touch with his own identity and to come to terms with the existential realities of current living. This challenge is put in a more profound way than the traditional responsibility of therapists' self-awareness. The proffered answers no doubt will be troubling to many. Second, he relates this existential reality to the new phenomenon—with which many therapists are acquainted—of clients who are experiencing the pains of alienation and are turning to therapists for help. This is a new type of problem for the therapist, one for which many thought systems do not have answers. Third, the author reminds therapists that without an awareness of the prevalence and manifestations of alienation there is a distinct risk that the very activities of the therapist can further alienate the client from himself and his significant others.

Everyone who reads this book will not agree with the author's view of professions and professional practice. But all readers should find important concepts that should enrich and strengthen psychotherapeutic practice in the decades ahead.

Francis J. Turner

Preface

Existential thought addresses the problem of alienation, commonly experienced in modern society in the form of self-doubt, dread, boredom, loneliness, self-preoccupation, guilt, anger, and anxiety. Efforts to deal with alienation take a variety of forms, including neurotic and psychotic symptoms, interpersonal games and experimentation, the pursuit of success and pleasurable or exciting distractions, the use or abuse of narcotics (drugs, alcohol, tobacco, etc.), and frenzied searches through books, the arts, growth groups, therapists, politicians, and philosophers for someone or something that can make it all better.

A basic premise of this book is that behind the problem of alienation is man's basic need for meaningful relation, for active engagement with life as it happens for him.* The developing theme of the book is the exploration of how alienation occurs and how it can be dealt with more effectively by helping professionals.

Helping professionals have been frustrated by their own lack of effectiveness in helping those whom they seek to help. The tendency has been to blame others: my approach is superior to yours; you are not dealing with the root of the problem. Therapists switch hopefully from one theory-treatment model to another; helpers move from clinic practice into social action or vice versa. Some minority professionals become disillusioned with the prospects of change offered by professional institutions and modes of functioning. We vacillate between guilty self-examination and anger at unyielding social forces.

*Throughout this book the terms "man" and "him" refer to both sexes, except where the context makes reference to a specific male person obvious.

xiii

From the existential perspective comes an intriguing hypothesis: the very way in which helping professionals pursue their efforts to change others may often be promoting alienation and thus aggravating the very problem they hope to solve. We are keenly aware that many segments of our society have invested us with the expectation of wisdom and know-how, and this complicates our own guilt and occasional rescuing frenzy.

In the opening chapter we will encounter the varied efforts of social workers to wrestle with the task of change. While the focus is upon social work, the same dynamics apply to other groups of helpers: psychiatrists, psychologists, nurses, probation officers, school counselors, ministers, and a variety of "paraprofessionals." It will become apparent that the several helping stances described are related to underlying philosophical positions. That of the "solitary"* reflects the existential perspective. While there will appear to be a bias in favor of the "solitary" position, therefore, I recognize that this, too, is an unverified assumption. My intent, as with most exponents of helping methods, is to highlight, clarify, and excite others toward new considerations of the helping role.

Chapters 2 and 3 deal with the issue of alienation by proposing two contrary views of experiencing (and believing in) personal identity. Ego identity, which has been the mainstay of the helping professions, is seen as a contributing force to the problem of alienation—within ourselves as well as with our client systems. The alternative, process identity, offers the possibility for vital engagement in the complexities of life and lends itself to a different emphasis upon the activity of change, which is explored later.

Chapters 4, 5, and 6 examine how some views of personality functioning are altered when considered from the existential philosophical position. A different view of pathology, or dysfunction, emerges as we see how varied life styles reflect different philosophical underpinnings. Not only our notions of dysfunction, but even our notions of health and maturity are called into question. This becomes the foundation for the "client-centered" perspective that permeates that existential approach to

---

*The existential social worker is characterizes by different labels throughout the book. This variation of labels is a deliberate attempt to highlight certain characteristics related to the context of a particular discussion. The "solitary" takes the form of the "masters-brothers of life" combination in Chapter 5. He appears as the "spontaneous strategist" in Chapter 8 and then as the "absurd social activist" in Chapter 11.

practice. It is this "client-centered" view that becomes the all-important countering force for the common tendency among helping professionals to be paternalistic guides and philosophical gurus.

The first half of the book builds a theoretical framework that not only sheds new light upon our understanding of clients but at the same time suggests a perspective for the therapist's understanding of himself. The major criticisms leveled at the social work profession refer to its authoritarianism, paternalism, intellectualism, and utopianism. Research efforts and experimental programs are sometimes suspect because of the bias expected from those who seem to have some axe to grind, some righteous rescue effort that must be accomplished, some prized theory that needs reassuring substantiation. These views reflect an identity insecurity, which haunts many helping professionals, not only social workers.

As the helping professional becomes disengaged from his personal anxieties, self-pity preoccupations, and hidden as well as outspoken resentments, he arrives at an inner void that permits a more responsive and creative engagement with the complex tasks that confront him in practice. It is the task of this book to explore the nature of this void, how one arrives there, and the pragmatic use one can make of this inner experience. Paradoxical as it may seem, the application of the existential stance to our understanding of practice in the helping professions provides for a flexibility, a detachment, an objectivity sorely needed today. The philosophy that had its birth in personal alienation results in an active, relational engagement with the problems of life.

The four chapters describing the activities of treatment emphasizes three principles. The first is the client-centered perspective mentioned above, which has implications for prognosis, diagnosis, goal setting, and sensitivity to the changing experience of the client from interview to interview.

The second point of emphasis is enhancing a client's rapid re-engagement with his own life circumstance. Change is viewed as a relational activity which recenters the client in his experience, his life process, rather than encourage self-alienating intellectual preoccupations or needless dependency upon the helper. This emphasis results in a new use of existential psychology that is particularly suited for social workers; namely, a present-focused interpersonal understanding of pathology and the change process. Previous writings on existential psychology have tended to emphasize intrapsychic understanding and exploration, which actually may contribute to the very problem of alienation that existentialists have hoped to relieve.

The third principle is the therapist's use of himself as artist–scientist. The therapist's way of dealing with his own image, feelings, and values affects his clients—sometimes obviously, more often subtly. It is important to understand this process, for it is inseparable from the often unrealistic expectations our clients place upon us. This is not simply a matter of "transference" but refers to the images of helping professionals posed by various social institutions (courts, physicians, churches, growth groups, the news media, art forms, welfare, etc.). To counteract therapy-inhibiting expectations, the therapist's role as "spontaneous strategist" is stressed. In this role he will often act in paradoxical ways and make eclectic use of therapy techniques so as to unbalance the very hopes, "hooks," and expectations of clients that impede the process of change. A most intriguing paradox utilized by both the clinician and the social activist has to do with one's view of change: change occurs in a most natural way when either one—therapist or client—alters the way he experiences what is happening.

In Chapter 11 we shall see how the existential view of change and the helper's use of himself are reflected in issues and challenges of social action. The "righteous reformer" tends to produce stubborn resistance in the very people he hopes to change, while at the same time instilling resentment and false hopes in the "victimized" group for whom he is the advocate. The "absurd social activist"—the existentialist—derives his personal satisfaction from his actions rather than his outcomes. In order to do this he must reshuffle his categorizations of "goods" and "evils."

The final chapter addresses some of the challenges and possibilities awaiting the social work profession. The existential model focuses upon social work's public and professional image, the place of research, and considerations for methods of professional education. I hope this ending will be a new beginning for many. The "greening of social work" (and of other helping professions) suggests a different perspective of reality and therefore a shift in creative energies as we seek to do our jobs and preserve our sanity in the process.

Existentialism has been challenged as a philosophy. Many people consider it to be a life stance rather than an organized system of philosophical concepts. The strict existentialist may be disheartened by the perspective developed here. I have emphasized such existential concepts as freedom of choice, the uniqueness of each person's subjective reality (being-in-the-world), "bad faith" as rigidified security images that impede growth, and engagement with present life experience for one's source of meaning. I have gone beyond the scope of the more pessimistic existentialists to include related philosophical perspectives associated with Zen Buddhism, Krishnamurti, and Carlos Castaneda.* This expansion not only broadens the cultural breadth of similar views of reality but also incorporates a more optimistic idea of modern man's struggle with the problem of alienation. This added dimension is not a departure from existentialism, for we find in the writings of the religious existentialists (Tillich, Buber, Kierkegaard, Marcel, Bardyaev) a link with the other perspectives incorporated here. This link is based on the subject of overcoming personal alienation by a rerooting in the life process itself. Such concepts as the "wisdom of the organism" and the possibility of "I-Thou" relations with our fellow men are common among the humanistic psychologies and are an outgrowth of this emphasis upon life-process engagement.

From the shifted view of reality, provided by the existential stance, there arises new formulations about the nature of health, pathology and the nature of change both with clients and social systems. This book is a beginning exploration of some of these exciting new directions.

---

*The most recent study of the writings of Carlos Castaneda is Richard DeMille's *Castaneda's Journey: The Power and the Allegory* (Santa Barbara, Calif.: Capra Press, 1976). DeMille concludes (as others have) that Castaneda's tales of Don Juan are fiction; nevertheless this does not detract from the wisdom and validity of Castaneda's vision of reality.

Acknowledgments

This book had its beginnings a decade ago, and over the years there have been many who contributed to its development. I wish to express my appreciation:

To the University of Denver for the funding made available to me for the preparation of the original manuscript and some subsequent revisions.

To the Graduate School of Social Work of the University of Denver, the students, staff, faculty, and Deans Emil Sunley and Kenneth Kindelsperger, all of whose responsiveness, interest, and service have been invaluable to me in producing this book.

To my wife, Lou, and friends who read and critiqued portions of the manuscript and lived patiently with my efforts of idea revision.

To my clients whose problems and struggles most effectively grounded many of my ideas in the reality of their human experience.

To the many scholars from whose wisdom I have drawn, many of whom are listed in the bibliography.

To the personal inspiration and influence upon my life direction of Wallace Fisher, Ezequiel Vieta, Ratibor Jurjevich, Donald Langsley, my parents, and my family.

Chapter 1

The Greening of Social Work

Who am I? Where am I going? What do I do next? These sound like the questions of an adolescent in quest of identity. But it is not only the young who raise these issues. And when they are raised by adults moving through middle age they stem from a different view of life. Instead of a rejection of the values of some authorities (parent, teacher, minister, advertiser), there is a questioning of one's own life style. With all my success, my satisfying relationships, my self-understanding, my commitment to noble causes, why am I lonely, dissatisfied, bored, and uneasy? And when one begins to question the validity of those purposes upon which he has spent his life energy, a profound fear and trembling arise that few young people can appreciate. The young more easily separate themselves from values they intellectually discern and then reject, for they can more easily move out into the awaiting world, experimenting with vitality and hope. The older adults have already finished their "hope trip," and they are at a significantly different point as they gaze into the abyss of alienation.

There are three dimensions to the problem of alienation: psychological, social, and spiritual. Elsewhere I have described how the psychological and social forces act upon one another to create "anomic man."[1] Briefly stated, man's psychological need for a sense of security and identity often conflicts with the growth responses within himself—realistic needs and potentials seeking

1

emergence. To act in a new way so as to fulfill such growth strivings is often risky, for it threatens an image he holds—an image that reminds him of his adequacy and/or lovableness. So men often sell out their own growth for security. They hold to values or beliefs that shore up this security image for fear of facing the insufficiency of these values. Ridden with guilt and anxiety, they seek escape from the knowledge of what they are doing to themselves.

Society supports the alienation process through seduction and oppression. Through seduction it provides people with a variety of oversimplified values that are naïve, materialistic, and/or egoistic. These values are readily adopted by people whose own security image requires additional support. The rugged he-man picks his models and the related merchandise, as does the playboy. It is not only the advertising media that provide seductive values for people. They are presented in films, novels, songs, churches. They are often given the apparent blessing of science in the "how to be happy" books of sexologists, psychologists, and the like. Society also acts to solidify the security images of many by oppression. Those who are already plagued with self-doubt may believe that their fate is sealed when they face the multifaceted forces of racial prejudice and segregation. This is outside confirmation for what they fearfully suspected about themselves.

But when the problem remains at the psychological-social level it appears remediable through social change and psychotherapy. It must be pushed further—into the spiritual dimension. At the spiritual or existential level, one realizes that answers and solutions are not easily forthcoming. The problem here appears to be that one may not be primarily alienated from one's self—from one's potentials and growth responses. Nor is one primarily alienated from other people, for one may have achieved a satisfying give and take with others. One may even have freed oneself successfully from those social forces that seek to penetrate his character and define who he is or should be. The problem here is that by the very fact that one has become a self-fulfilling individual he has also opened himself to an experiencing of existence that is frightening. The existentialists call it dread. That which is experienced is nothingness, the hole, emptiness.

What is dread? A friend recently shared with me the following reflections about himself:

> I have been rather lucky in my forty years of life—no severe setbacks with job, health, or marriage. Our three children are coming along nicely. My marriage is settled and we have a close-ness and a decent understanding. We've made good friendships and are a vital part of our community. My job has been personally fulfilling. I have time for sports and other relaxations. I completed a successful psychoanalysis several years ago and now have gone the route of experimenting with encounter groups, meditation, a few drugs, and done extensive reading in philosophy and theol-ogy. I am generally an aware and open person. I keep learning from experiences such as these, and I have been involved with social action, too—the peace movement and civil rights.
>
> But I must tell you an awful secret, and after I tell you I don't want any advice from you. Just listen, please. In spite of all this, I feel a lack. When the activities cease and the commotion clears away and I am alone with nothing particular to do or think about—then it comes like a black hole. At first it is boredom, then like a minor depression. But if I stay with it there grows this tremendous sense of a lack. And lack of what I don't know. How shall I fill it: travel? affairs? a new hobby or sport? expanding my professional skills? another just cause? partying? No—all these seem to be futile gestures. Some of them have meaning for me, but it is a temporary and situational meaning. They do not fill the hole. I am also tired of whipping myself with "oughts" and "shoulds." I am relatively happy with myself. What is this emptiness—this lack? Don't answer, for if you have an answer it means you don't understand me.

How widespread is this feeling? It is difficult to estimate. If one considered such symptoms as divorce rate, use of tranquiliz-ers, the rising number of depressed middle-aged people consult-ing psychotherapists, the generation gap (as a reaction of the young to what they perceive to be empty values in their parents' lives), one could conclude that it pervades middle-class society.

How people react to the experience of dread may vary widely. The friend quoted above was seeking a kind of personal lucidity in relation to his experience. He preferred this to escape efforts. There was also an attraction, a curiosity in his attitude—as someone gaining a glimpse of death and uneasily seeking a closer look.

There are those who accept the reality of dread but seek to control its effect upon them by countering it with fulfilling activities. Some do this by seeking as many "uplifting," or "turned on" experiences as possible—travel, sports, drugs, adventure, affairs, encounter groups, psychotherapy, religious retreats, etc. This is a kind of holding action by utilizing valued life experiences. In this sense they maintain a lucidity that escapes those who seek the diversions of alcohol, tranquilizers, a drive to activity, marriage switching, and passive entertainment—but without knowing what it is they are running from.

Another group consists of those who see the reality of dread but rebel against its meaning. They conclude that dread reveals the essential absurdity and chaos of the universe. Since all is senseless anyway, one might as well seek out what is pleasurable and pleasing to oneself and do it as often as there is energy to do so (Albert Ellis). Or, more humanistically, one may affirm the drive to live in oneself as well as in others despite the final absurdity of it all (Albert Camus). This affirmation of life in spite of absurdity has both heroic and passionate ingredients. For Camus, the very awareness of the absurd reveals to man his own freedom and dignity. He is not a puppet of fate. He chooses who he is. Even in the face of fate, suffering, and death, man still chooses his own attitude toward them (Viktor Frankl). Awareness of the absurd, for Camus, also results in human solidarity that is characterized by individual freedom and justice. For if there are no absolutes, then no tyrant is justified in oppressing any man. And under the shadow of an ultimately absurd existence, people are bound together in compassion for one another.

Then there are religious responses to dread. A formerly common but no longer popular attitude was that man experiences such suffering in this world because he is essentially alien to it—he will find his home in whatever reality awaits him after death. In recent years religion has emphasized a more intimate God, one who is somehow involved in the daily experiences of men. Religious existentialists, in particular, have considered the experience of dread to be a revealing experience. Nothingness and Being are inseparable—two sides of the same coin. The yin-yang symbol of Buddhism speaks to this same insight. Christ reveals the contrasting experiences of life in two sayings: "My God, my God, why hast thou forsaken me?" and "Nevertheless, not my will but thine be done." The dread of nothingness revealed to Kierkegaard a different dimension to reality which he called the absolute Telos. Tillich dealt extensively with this experience as the source of one's "courage to be." For Tillich this experience of meaninglessness, when accepted with lucidity, could result in an experiential faith. One found oneself affirmed by the "power of Being" in this very moment of disillusionment or estrangement from one's usual ego supports. The act of courage—to go on with life—accepting the nothingness experience as a part of the whole life process, is in itself a living out of the undergirding power that affirms life as meaningful even when in the clutches of radical despair.

The mystic goes a step farther. He makes a companion of dread. He deliberately courts the nothingness experience in order to penetrate it. Here is the Dark Night of the Soul, for St. John of the Cross, and the No-Mind of Zen. Meditation is the actual effort to reroot oneself in this Nothingness by being wholly in touch with the reality of the moment—presence without mental meanderings and distractions. When the mystic penetrates dread he speaks of his experience in words that are unintelligible to the rational mind: Nothingness is also the All; caprice and chaos equal meaningful relation; emptiness is fulfillment. The paradoxical irrationality of such statements stems from the experience itself, which dissolves the self/other dichotomy (as we ordinarily experience the world surrounding our own identified ego) and results in a realization of unity (the Satori experience in Zen).

A story of Chuang Tzu, the Chinese Taoist, reveals this position:

> There was a man who was so disturbed by the sight of his own shadow and so displeased with his own footsteps that he determined to get rid of both. The method he hit upon was to run away from them.
>
> So he got up and ran. But every time he put his foot down there was another step, while his shadow kept up with him without the slightest difficulty.
>
> He attributed his failure to the fact that he was not running fast enough. So he ran faster and faster, without stopping, until he finally dropped dead.
>
> He failed to realize that if he merely stepped into the shade, his shadow would vanish, and if he sat down and stayed still, there would be no more footsteps.[2]

Then there are those people who are acquainted with the dread experience, but who refuse to accept it as an inevitable part of the human condition. They view dread as being psychologically, socially, or economically caused. With more education, more social science, more opportunities, more wealth, more scientific control over nature, more genuine and close human relationships, dread could be overcome. Dread is man-made and therefore can be extinguished by the efforts of man. The future of society and civilization is their hope. This position is a bedfellow of rationalism and utopianism.

Charles Reich's book *The Greening of America* proposes a shifting of consciousness within the United States—from Consciousness I (rugged individualism) to Consciousness II (rational organizationalism) to Consciousness III (heightened individual awareness). Each consciousness represents a philosophy of living with its implications for every aspect of society—the economic system, politics, military, education, family, social relationships, beliefs about one's own nature, and so forth. Reich sees a historical evolution of consciousness occurring within the United States from its time of constitutional origin until now. His descriptions of Consniousness II seem frequently accurate for the leadership that has characterized much of the social work profession ever since the 1930s. It is the youth culture of recent years which supplies Reich's description of the new life style and values that exemplify Consciousness III. The optimistic message of Reich's book is that older people who have been dominated by either Consciousness I or Consciousness II attitudes can shift to a Consciousness III position as they become increasingly aware of how they are being dehumanized by the present mode of society's operation. The revolution, if necessary, does not involve violent political overthrow, but rather a philosophical version that will in turn change one's life style. Such a shift can subsequently have profound effects upon the whole operation of the social-political-economic system.[3]

Reich's thesis has been questioned by many, particularly his negative judgments about Consciousness II life style and what appears to be an exaggerated optimism about the meaning and future of the Consciousness III life style.[4] These considerations aside, Reich does propose a view of change that can have useful implications for social work. The "Greening of Social Work," like the "Greening of America," could result from a shift in personal (and related social) philosophies with a concomitant alteration in life styles. Professionally we have already sensed this happening with the "new breed" of social work students and young practitioners. In social work we have sometimes viewed this change as a gradual polarization between young "activists" and older "traditionalists," even though the issue of age is almost irrelevant. This dichotomy has implied that there are the service-oriented workers concerned about helping specific individuals and families with their day-to-day problems of living, and there are the community-oriented workers who prefer to put their efforts into effecting change in the systems at large, involving themselves more directly in causal factors of poverty, crime, racism, emotional disturbance, and the like.

This is an erroneous oversimplification, for there are divergent philosophical positions among both "activists" and "traditionalists." Much of our difficulty with professional polarizations, suspicions, and backbiting may be related to our failure to differentiate the varied kinds of professional social workers we are as people. Instead we do battle with one another over theories and modes of intervention that on the surface separate us. A more careful understanding of our personal philosophical differences can result in more of a mutual acceptance and respect for one another as professionals. There is a need for variety in personal and philosophical standpoints. Such social work types as the impulsive helper, the mechanical conformist, the rational organizer, the solid plodder, the rebel, and the solitary may operate as either "traditionalists" or "activists." What differentiates them primarily are their beliefs about the meaning of life, the human condition, one's own private destiny, and their expectations for human relationships.

Social Work Types

The "impulsive helper" is rooted primarily in feelings. This commitment through feelings is primarily narcissistic, for his helping behavior supports, shores up, reassures his own self-worth and sense of adequacy. He uses others (even under the guise of helping them) as a means to prove his own adequacy. The impulsive helper has never learned discipline. He does not know how to listen to life outside of himself.

The impulsive helper often appears as a "bleeding heart" or else a "cry of protest," righteously indignant over the suffering of the world. Behind his anger at "punitive authorities," whether they are politicians, teachers, police, or parents, is commonly the thinly disguised wish to be an authority oneself—the good authority who will make up for all the bad ones as he "lovingly" directs the lives of people. And we can see this "benevolent authoritarianism'' in all areas of social work practice, including some of those called the "new breed" of activists.

The "mechanical conformist" has little interest or understanding about the central tasks of the profession. He lives off the profession by operating as a mechanical cog in some aspect of its bureaucratic structure. He is commonly found doing administrative tasks that often could be better done by computers or clerks. His activity as a helper is mechanical and unimaginative. His behavior tends to reinforce the public image of the inept social worker and he resists any effort toward change of the bureaucratic structure that might require him to acquire some talent and sensitivity. He is bound by his pocketbook and job security. The "mechanical conformist" resembles the "impulsive helper" in his self-centeredness. He differs in that he seldom wears the disguise of a "committed helper." The mechanical conformist tends to be authoritative, too, because he is determined to maintain the status quo.

The "rational organizer" is a different brand of social work authoritarian. He is not usually rooted in his own egoism. He views himself as a scientist, and he is devoted to a philosophy of rationalism. He believes that man makes his world and that the sufferings of the world can be overcome through proper education and the use of reason. He views himself as essentially objective in outlook and genuinely seeks to improve society through education and the careful application of knowledge. He abhors what appears chaotic, irrational, unverifiable, uncontrollable. His strength is in conceptualization, data gathering, and integration of knowledge. His weakness lies in his failure to understand and respond when life itself defies his categories and prescriptions. At such moments his capacity for self-deception through intellectualization is tremendous. He tends to absolutize his theories whether he is psychoanalytic, a learning theorist, or a molder of communities.

The "solid plodder" occupies a middle position. He is relatively free of egotistical concerns. His hope for rational knowledge is balanced by a healthy respect for its limitations. While he senses the intensity of feeling in others, he is hesitant to join their passions or apparent irrationality. He is a pragmatist. He wants to know what works and what does not. He is, therefore, interested in research and cautious experimentation. The solid plodder sees constructive change coming gradually and hesitantly through the legal, political, and professional systems. He benefits from the knowledge and research provided by the rational organizer. He is likewise impressed and appreciative of the emotional involvement of other social work types. He is not easily deceived by the impulsive helper and is often able to redirect his efforts into more constructive channels. From this standpoint, the solid plodder is probably the most effective social work administrator.

The "rebel" is a dissatisfied leader. He is genuinely committed. He wants to change a portion of the world, and he knows what must be different. He is willing to take the risks necessary. He knows there are others who fight for the same ends and that they will take up the struggle if he fails. He has a cause that is right and brethren by his side. His professional commitment is often restricted to that area of life he vitally knows and in which he seeks change.

The "solitary" is a lone seeker. He, too, is committed. He wants to understand life so as to go with it and not against it. He, too, experiences risks, for he seeks a confrontation with unknowns—with the flux, the chaos, and the silences of life. Suffering and death and meaninglessness are his brethren; so, too, are wonder and alertness and compassion. His own identity is of questionable consequence. Of all the types mentioned, the solitary best understands the alienation and anomie that pervade modern middle-class society. He does not have clear answers to these problems, but he has learned how to listen and how to live with ambiguities.*

*The solitary is most clearly characterized in Thomas Merton's *Disputed Questions,* "Notes for a Philosophy of Solitude" (New York: Mentor-Omega, 1960), pp. 139–60. The solitary is a sort of spiritual wanderer. While Merton's description is essentially a religious one, the concept can also be understood in nonreligious terminology as it is found in Zen and existentialism. The character of the solitary is given major attention here because it seems the least understood by most social workers. The other four categories of social workers have been arbitrarily conceived as a means of providing contrast to the rebel and the solitary.

Let us consider some implications of the activities of this array of characters in the drama of social work. These six categories need not be seen in some hierarchical ladder of importance. Rather, they fit around the perimeter of a circle. Each has its place. The rebel and the solitary provide a balance to the rational organizer and the impulsive helper. The rational organizer and solid plodder will struggle successfully with certain problems that neither the rebel nor the solitary would wish to take upon themselves. The impulsive helper will sometimes risk himself in creative or rebellious gestures that will have constructive results despite his egoistic motives. And what he tries may be unthinkable for any of the other types mentioned. Even the mechanical conformist has a place. The profession may wish to be less bureaucratic and may find itself embarrassed by the robotlike behavior of some of its representatives. But someone must do these jobs until the structure changes, and some useful purposes are served by the present system in spite of its many faults and failures.

On the other hand, how much power or influence is given to these types may be of critical concern for the social work profession. The direction of the profession is at stake here. I would suggest a few unverified speculations. In terms of numbers, there are more solid plodders, mechanical conformists, and impulsive helpers than any other grouping. The power of influence in the profession has for many years resided with the rational organizers and the impulsive helpers. The rebels are a smaller group but are growing in number and in the last few years have made significant inroads. The solitary is least in number and has had little impact upon the concerns of the profession. He is the least understood yet a most important potential influence for the "Greening of Social Work." The rebel will also have a critical role in this "greening" process, although his vision is somewhat more restricted than that of the solitary.

In order to grasp how the "Greening of Social Work" can occur, it will be important to better understand the characters of the rebel and the solitary. The rebel has already made himself known rather effectively through journal writings on minority issues, social action, and advocacy as well as by tactics of confrontation with fellow professionals. Since the solitary is relatively unknown, he will be developed in some detail.

The six social work types described are seldom found in their pure state. There is often an overlapping or combination of categories within the same person. The solid plodder may at times believe and behave as a rational organizer or as a rebel and then return to his solid plodder perspective. The solitary may at times behave like an impulsive helper. We are talking about philosophical stances, but a philosophical stance is sometimes temporarily altered by a mood or a passion; and sometimes a stance is shifted in a more permanent way. Even the rebel may not necessarily be a minority person or someone rooted in poverty himself. There can be WASP rebels who have experienced tyranny or oppression in more subtle forms, but who know it well just the same and can lead others to oppose oppression in whatever form it may take. And, needless to say, most of us have operated as mechanical conformists at times.

The Rebel and the Solitary

Neither the rebel nor the solitary identifies with the established order. Both see its superficiality and deceptions; neither is willing to sell out his commitment to truth, honesty, and justice. Both understand the seductive and oppressive forces at work in society (and among professionals) to induce conformity and adjustment to a faulty order.

Both the rebel and the solitary are irrationalists insofar as they say: Let life speak for itself and let us listen first and then respond, instead of seeking to shape life according to our intellectual speculations. Neither group puts much stock in what many psychological and sociological theorists deterministically proclaim man to be or what they claim he should be made into. Both groups are in touch with the movement of life, not dominated by theories. They suspect the aloof intellectual with his careful planning, his superior knowledgeability of the needs of others.

Abraham Maslow's idea of a need hierarchy provides an explanation for some important differences between the rebel and the solitary.[5] People tend to experience life from different perspectives depending upon the need awareness most prominent to them. Need-awareness levels progress upward from the physical to safety, to social, to ego, to self-actualization. The idea is that people dominated by physical or safety need-awareness will have little comprehension of a need level beyond their own. They may know that others in society are greatly concerned with finding their place in a world of other people, understanding their inner conflicts, or realizing their potentials. But these concerns will seem superficial to a person who is hungry, cold, or worried about simply being able to live without coercion and harm. The life perspective of many rebels is dominated by physical, safety, and social need-awareness. They speak for others (commonly minorities) who are deprived in these areas. Justice and opportunity are principal concerns.

In contrast, the other social-work types, with the exception of the solitary, appear to be dominated by the ego and self-actualization need-awareness levels. This is an important reason why the social work profession for so long has been ineffective in dealing with needs and problems of the poor and minority groups. This is also why minority leaders have stressed the importance of minority people speaking for themselves as to the definition of their needs, problems, and directions. The source of confusion here is not that white middle-class social workers fail to understand the poor and the minorities because they are living on a different need-awareness level. Often such social workers have an openness and a sensitivity to such problems that are quite accurate. The problem has had to do much more with the subtle authoritarianism of social workers (especially the impulsive help-ers, mechanical conformists, and rational organizers) that seeks to force their own values on others. They wish to inspire, seduce, and cajole others to change and adjust to a need-awareness level that is foreign to them. The fact of the matter is that there is little choice involved in changing from one need-awareness level to another. It simply happens spontaneously when one need level is sufficiently relieved or gratified. Whether one wants to move up the hierarchy from one level to another or to bring someone else up the ladder is of little consequence. Movement up the ladder simply occurs when the time comes.

The perspective of the solitary has similarities to the self-actualization need level; yet there are differences. If a new cate-gory were to be added for the solitary it would be *Logo*-awareness. The solitary understands a tragic fact about man: as people move from one category of need awareness to another, suffering is not overcome but simply takes a new form. He knows that, if the rebels succeed in helping the masses to realize a higher life style, they will soon be suffering from the same anomie, the same sense of personal alienation, and the same egotistical con-cerns that now dominate the more affluent classes. The rebel tends not to believe this, for he remains in the grip of enormous hopes for a future yet to be determined. His reply to the solitary is that such alienation will not occur because alienation results from a faulty society built upon oppression and deception.

And so the rebel and the solitary are often in different camps. The solitary acknowledges the validity of the rebel's concern, but he knows that life can be lived meaningfully at any need-awareness level—each has its own particular joys and sufferings. He also values the development of each person's humanity—his creative uniqueness as a person and his outreach to his fellow man. The solitary recognizes that there is greater opportunity for this to occur as people move higher up the need-level ladder.

But the solitary sees the scope of social work as including and going beyond the concerns of the rebel. Social work is also ac-tively struggling with the problems of an alienated middle class. If it fails to maintain its involvement with this level of social-psychological-spiritual need it will be unprepared to give effective service to formerly underprivileged groups when they make entry into the "advantages and opportunities" of the majority culture. The rebels will be of little help in the present effort of dealing with middle-class alienation, for their very life perspective cannot appreciate the complexities of this problem. Even with the possibility of radical changes in the social-political-economic structure, the solitary believes the alienation problem will persist when people move to higher levels of need awareness.

The rebel suspects this logic, for it sounds too much like that of the liberal rationalists, with whom he is familiar. His own life perspective says that talk of life's meaning is often aristocratic self-indulgence, a way of avoiding the genuine and concrete needs of masses of people in pain. Perhaps this is an unfair judgment against the solitary, however, because the solitary has no particular stake in the continuation of an unjust system, and he remains actively in touch with the sufferings of humanity.

There is often a difference in professional goals between the rebel and the solitary. The rebel sees the most critical objective to be help for the minority or underprivileged group with which he is identified. More broadly, he may see the goal as elimination of oppression, poverty, and segregation everywhere, so that genuine justice might prevail. The solitary would accept this goal, although he would probably substitute "reduction" for "elimination." But the solitary is concerned with a more particular goal—the humanization of the social work profession. Social work must seek to reduce the forces of dehumanization among all groups of people (including social workers). And social work's response to the troubles of modern middle-class America is an important consideration. The problem of anomie, of meaninglessness, of alienation may not simply be the result of a society that some would call bigoted and oppressive. It might just as well be true that a society remains bigoted and oppressive in its efforts to defend against the pain of alienation and meaninglessness!

The rebel tends toward activism, using power tactics and confrontation. The solitary tends toward reflective contemplation. He is interested in heightening self-awareness, in helping others tune in to the messages of their lives so as to be more fully human. And he wishes to join them as a fellow human being immersed in the same struggle for meaning.

The solitary can appreciate the passion of the rebel, for the rebel is the fire in the midst of the oppressed confronting their oppressors—whether this is within a community, an agency, or a university. The detachment of the solitary, combined with his level of need awareness, has often taken him beyond the passionate stance of the rebel. Insofar as this is true, he depends upon the rebel for leadership, boldness, and the charisma that is often necessary to stir others to legitimate change efforts.

On the other hand, the very fire that drives the rebel and brightens his focus of concern also restricts his vision. There are shades and shadows along the perimeter of his firelight that he fails to comprehend. The solitary is more a man of the dark, the shadows, and can supply broader perspectives to the rebel when needed. It is the solitary who is well acquainted with the limits, the contradictions, the self-deceptions, the paradoxes of human nature and society.

Who Is the Solitary?

Through exposure to dread, the sotitary has tasted an intuitive kind of wisdom. Like Sidhartha or Zorba, the solitary listens to life as to a musical score, and his activity is that of a dance. As instruments, notes, players combine to produce music, which itself is the rhythm of sounds and silences, so it is with the variety of people, the trees and the seas, ideas and efforts, and one's own inner responses to it all.

The solitary has learned to listen. And in listening he has realized that there is little to proclaim. He aids the listening of others and, like a midwife, allows life to emerge in them in whatever unique manner it happens. He realizes that what may appear irrational and foreign to him may hold profound meaning to another. His task is to learn and expand his knowledge through the opening up of genuine contacts. And the most profound truth he has learned can better be shown by what he does than by what he professes.

There is a certain detachment in the solitary. He possesses the heart of the footloose, wandering poet. There is a placid center within him that can withstand the turbulence and contradictions of daily life. While this center can make him fearless in the face of threat, it also emanates compassion and care for all forms of life. He is not easily deceived by the superficial values paraded by a society that seeks to use men as instruments.

The solitary appreciates the power and the many faces of evil and deception in the world. He is alert to the egoistic dictator who would seek to control and contain life for his own ends. And he sees this not only in the politician, the policeman, the bureaucrat, and the military man, but in the teacher, the helping professional, the idealistic leader of ''just movements,'' the student, and in himself. He knows that effective confrontation with such forces requires a well-rooted discipline.

Life is understood by the solitary through its tears and laughter, its beauty and troubles, and in its awesome mystery. What we put together in theories and conceptualizations are pitiable yet noble efforts to convey that which cannot be fully comprehended. And when one is genuinely in touch with the meandering river that is life, the conceptualizations are unnecessary.

The Solitary Perspective

What is it the solitary has come to understand? He has looked into the abyss of nothingness, and in contrast to some of the reactions to dread we have mentioned the solitary chooses not to escape, not to rebel, not to ignore, and not to deny.

Thomas Merton describes the solitary as follows:

He is called to emptiness. And in this emptiness, he does not find points upon which to base a contrast between himself and others. On the contrary, he realizes, though perhaps confusedly, that he has entered into a *solitude that is really shared by everyone*. It is not that he is solitary while everybody else is social: but that everyone is solitary, in a solitude masked by the symbolism which they use to cheat and counteract their solitariness. What the solitary renounces is not his union with other men, but rather the deceptive fictions and inadequate symbols which tend to take the place of genuine social unity—to produce a facade of apparent unity without really uniting men on a deep level [emphasis in original].[6]

There are two aspects of the emptiness experience. One is negative and painful, while the other is positive and intuitively enlightening. The negative reactions are characterized at times as dread, fear and trembling, anxiety, nausea, outrage, melancholy, despair, sadness, and radical loneliness. The positive descriptions speak of joy, unity, illumination, love, compassion, alertness, humor, wonder, and peace. And these two opposing reactions are interrelated.

Don Quixote was confronted by a vast lake of boiling pitch in which all sorts of fearsome creatures wallowed about. A voice beckoned him on saying that if he were ever to realize the wonders for which he searched he must hurl himself into these murky waters. No sooner did the voice cease than Don Quixote rushed into the boiling lake. Then, just as he did not know what was happening to him, he found himself in beautiful flowery fields.[7]

Herman Hesse's Steppenwolf, an example of alienated man in our present society, is admonished by Mozart in his fanciful experience with "the magic theater":

You are to live and to learn to laugh. You are to learn to listen to the cursed radio music of life and to reverence the spirit behind it and to laugh at its distortions. So there you are. More will not be asked of you.[8]

A listening and attunement are called for by the solitary. But this is not to be taken as a life of passivity. The Samurai warriors of Japan commonly were followers of Zen. They believed that in order to be most keenly alert and prepared for whatever action might be called forth, one had to face nothingness. One had to die first to his usual ego preoccupations, worries, and judgments in order to be fully in the moment at hand. As one becomes increasingly detached from such ego concerns he arrives at a state of "pure awareness" or "presence." He is not threatened by the caprice and happenstance of life, for he experiences himself as a part of the very irrational movement of life itself. He is no more attached to nothingness and peace than he is to action and fulfillment. Both are of the order of existence.

Gestalt psychology suggests a similar view of human experience. The person is a process of emerging and dissolving gestalts. A gestalt consists of a figure (focused foreground) and a ground (background). The human process of experiencing is that of awareness of arising excitements with focus and potential for interaction with one's surroundings. But it is also the returning to rest, to peace, to nothingness, wherein one is not aware of one's individual potentials, limits, and so forth. One simply is. There is relation and connectedness; there is silence and emptiness. The former continually arise out of the latter. And while the silence of nothingness is beyond any subject/object differentiation, it is no less a manner of being, a genuine experience of reality. For the solitary to come to understand, accept, and even love this nothingness—as a rootedness, a recurring centering—is every bit as important as loving the moments of relation and fulfillment. Perhaps it is even more important, for in the experience of nothingness one transcends the sense of isolation as he participates in that which is the ground of every form of existence. In such moments, one realizes, too, that the negative reactions to nothingness stem from the mental flurry of ego concerns and not from nothingness itself.

The chapters that follow are an elaboration upon the perspective and activity of the solitary. We shall come to understand how he experiences reality and the way in which such experiencing gives him the necessary detachment to deal with the complexities of people's problems. We shall see how his reverence for the uniqueness of each person provides him with a heightened sensitivity to tyrannical and authoritative maneuvers of "helping" professionals. We shall discover an interesting paradox: the solitary's very ability to abandon both fear and hope in relation to his own ego strivings results in a more hopeful, affirming stance in relation to his clients. The solitary appreciates the many faces of alienation, for he has faced up to his own experience of it. (He even sees how the very efforts of many helping professionals actually promote alienation in their clients.) Yet he has passed beyond self-pity, for he has discovered at the very heart of the alienation experience the possibility of rebirth of relation, of meaningful connection, of full life-affirmation. In this very affirmation he renders to his clients a necessary experiential gift.

Notes

1. Donald F. Krill, "Existential Psychotherapy and the Problem of Anomie," *Social Work,* April 1969, pp. 33–49.

2. Thomas Merton, *The Way of Chuang Tzu* (New York: New Directions, 1965), pp. 155.

3. Charles Reich, *The Greening of America* (New York: Random House, 1970).

4. Philip Nobile, ed., *The Con III Controversy: The Critics Look at the Greening of America* (New York: Pocket Books, 1971).

5. Frank Goble, *The Third Force* (New York: Pocket Books, 1971), pp. 37–53.

6. Thomas Merton, *Disputed Questions* (New York: Mentor-Omega, 1960), pp. 146–47.

7. R. H. Blyth, *Zen in English Literature and Oriental Classics* (New York: E. P. Dutton, 1960), pp. 204–5.

8. Herman Hesse, *Steppenwolf* (New York: Holt, Rinehart & Winston, 1963), p. 216.

Chapter 2

Process Identity and Ego Identity

It is one thing to describe the characteristics of the solitary with reference to his perspective on reality. It is quite another matter to examine in some detail how his views are similar to and different from the theories about personality functioning currently popular among the helping professions. An important task of the professional helper is to integrate his subjective experience of life with his developing philosophy or religion. These must then become compatible with whatever personality or social theory undergirds his practice. This integration becomes his base of personal power, the source of his influence in his helping role.

The strategies and techniques of the helping professions are an outgrowth of psychological and social theories. These theories in turn are based on varied philosophical propositions about the nature of man, the purpose of life, and the meaning of human existence. A shortcoming in the teaching of psychological and social theories is its frequent failure to examine the philosophical underpinnings and how they are reflected in the helping strategies related to theories. In this chapter and the following three we shall be examining basic precepts of existential thought as well as some closely related philosophical influences from Buddhism, Christianity, Judaism, and American Indian thought. We shall discover a critically important departure from the traditional ego-rooted philosophies that have dominated the helping profession.

A wide variety of thinkers are associated with the existential camp. Some, like Kierkegaard, Nietzsche, and Dostoevski, never knew they would someday be termed "existentialist." Others, like Martin Heidegger, have rejected the label completely. They include atheists: Jean-Paul Sartre, Albert Camus, Simone de Beauvoir; Jews: Martin Buber, Franz Rosenzweig; Catholics: Jacques Maritain, Gabriel Marcel; Protestants: Paul Tillich, Reinhold Niebuhr; Russian Orthodox: Nicholas Berdyaev; and some with no clear place on the religion-atheist spectrum, such as Heidegger and Nikos Kazantzakis.

Similarities between existential thinking and Oriental religious thought have been alluded to by such authors as Thomas Merton, Erich Fromm, Fritz Perls, D. T. Suzuki, Paul Watzlawick, Ram Dass, and Alan Watts. Zen Buddhism is most often mentioned in this regard. The teachings of Krishnamurti, easily integrated with Zen thought, are another source. Sam Keen has pointed out similarities between existential and Zen thought and the writings of Carlos Castaneda in his development of the Yaqui "way of knowledge."[1]

This expanded version of existential thought, integrating the perspectives of the religious existentialists with Oriental and American Indian thought, seems more optimistic in thrust than the gloom usually expected from existentialists. I have called this perspective "process-rooted" because of its emphasis on man's need and ability to transcend his ordinary ego-alienated consciousness and experience himself as a part of some comprehensive, meaningful process. Whether this is called God or Void or Nagual or Suchness or Tao or the Nature of Things makes little difference. This view is in contrast to the perspective of man as having turned up in an absurd universe with his own mind (ego) as the only hope for the construction of a meaningful or happy life for himself and others. This we can call the "ego-rooted" stance.

We come to appreciate the complexity of life through paradoxical descriptions of activity. The use of paradox is common in religious writings such as Zen stories, the Hassidic Tales of

Judaism, and the teachings of Christ. Yet to the pragmatic mind of the modern helping professional, the messages in some of these teachings tend toward the outrageous.

Haquin was a Zen priest who lived in a small village and was reputed by villagers to live a pure life. His hut was not far from a food store. The lovely daughter of the store owner discovered herself pregnant one day. Under her parents' pressure she finally reported that the child's father was Haquin. When the parents confronted Haquin, his only comment was, "Is that so?"

After the child was born it was presented to Haquin. Though his reputation in the village was now destroyed, he willingly accepted the child and cared for it. A year later the parents came to Haquin again. Their daughter had admitted that the father really was a young man who worked in the local fish market. The parents begged Haquin's forgiveness. He willingly returned the child to them, and his only comment was, "Is that so?"[2]

Herman Hesse conveys the following world view through his fictional character, Siddhartha:

Within Siddhartha there slowly grew and ripened the knowledge of what wisdom really was and the goal of his long seeking. It was nothing but the preparation of the soul, a capacity, a secret art of thinking, feeling, and breathing thoughts of unity at every moment of life.

... Therefore, it seems to me [said Siddhartha] that everything that exists is good—death as well as life, sin as well as holiness, wisdom as well as folly. Everything is necessary, everything needs only my agreement, my assent, my loving understanding; then all is well with me and nothing can harm me. I learned through my body and soul that it was necessary for me to sin, that I needed lust, that I had to strive for propriety, and experience nausea and the depths of despair in order to learn not to resist them, in order to learn to love the world, and no longer compare it with some kind of desired, imaginary world, some imaginary vision of perfection, but to leave it as it is, to love it and be glad to belong to it.[3]

What is it that rankles us in these messages? There is a profound affirmation of life as it is, an acceptance of the bad with the good, of suffering valued as much as joy. Many of us continue to identify human happiness with material comfort, security, the achievement of power and status, or the satisfaction of pleasure "needs." Even our social reformers seek to bring about a new and good society where these needs will be satisfied for everyone.

Jesus described those who enter the Kingdom of God as being humble-minded, the bearers of sorrow and suffering, empty of personal positions. He taught nonresistance to those who would do you harm and a caring for one's enemies. When, late in his life, Leo Tolstoy underwent a religious conversion and decided to model these teachings of Jesus in his daily life, many thought him to be mad.

What troubles us about such thinking? There appears to be a violation of the very service commitment we follow as helping professionals. We seek to alleviate or at least reduce suffering. We know that in order to do this we need to gain some position of power in this world so as to counteract the many forces causing human misery. Control is necessary; weak passivity is self-defeating!

There is a Zen tale of two men riding horseback for several days en route to a distant city. Finally they crossed a hilltop from which they could see the city sprawling below them. The younger man set his horse into a gallop with a shout of joy. When he noticed his older companion still walking his horse at a leisurely pace, he stopped and shouted back, "Come on, let's go!" The older man replied, "It is good here, too."[4]

Whatever is before you is sufficient unto itself. Washing the dishes is just as important (or unimportant) as performing a surgical operation. Jesus admonished people for their constant worry and concern about self-evaluation. He suggested, instead, they look to the birds and the flowers, which simply exist as they are.

We find such thinking alien to what we know people need: lives of self-fulfillment, of more peak experiences, of more validation of personal adequacy through achievement. Happiness is just around the corner, on that next peak following the inevitable preparation and planful effort to get there. Self-actualization requires assertiveness, hope, planning, excitement. Where would socity be today if people had been satisfied with dishrags, bows, and hand plows?

Roger Blythe, describing Zen's poetic sense of unity in the nature of things, of life as it flows, wrote the following:

> When it rains, it is God's will, and God's will is my will, God's rain is my rain. Thus it is my rain that rains, it is my own specially ordered rain that wets me to the skin and chills me to the marrow, gives me consumption and kills me. It is my sun that shines, it is my time that silvers my hair by my request, loosens my teeth at my command. This is the faith, the love, that moves the sun and the other stars, and the mountains as well.[5]

There is a disturbing implication here that each of us is totally responsible for what happens to us. This notion is further expounded by Dostoevski's saintly character, Father Zossima:

> There is only one means of salvation, then take yourself and make yourself responsible for all men's sins, that is the truth, you know, friends, for as soon as you sincerely make yourself responsible for everything and for all men, you will see at once that it is really so, and that you are to blame for everyone and for all things.[6]

Dostoevski's view of life was that not only man's sin but his acts of love and forgiveness were universal in their effect upon both nature and human life.

The height of masochism and grandiosity! We have been outraged by Jesus' claim that sin is not only in the act of adultery but in the very thought of it. As if such an irrational incitement of man's guilt were not enough, we find that man is totally responsible for the pain and suffering of the world!

We have modeled our visions of man on a very different basis from the religious-philosophical perspectives suggested above. We have even used our "psychological insights" to discredit religious thought. Freud would have us view religion as an illusion, a defense. And we have been left with our lonely but rational egos.

Process Identity

There is a view of human functioning that sees validity in these paradoxical perspectives. The ever central concern about human identity is rooted in the sense one makes out of his experience. Is reality out there, in here, in both places, in neither place? "What is reality?" is the flip side of the question "Who am I?" Fortunately, we have permitted and encouraged an expansion of psychological and social theory in recent years so that the description that follows is compatible with knowledge development in the social sciences. In Chapter 6 we will look at the theories of Jung, Maslow, and Boss and at gestalt and systems theory as they relate to our philosophical perspective.

In Figure 2-1, the solid oval represents the field of interacting life processes, incorporating "outer" as well as "inner" activities. The subjective realization of this view of self/world (being-in-the-world) has been described as Quality (Pirsig), no-mind and suchness (Zen), seeing (Castaneda), God's will, grace, God as both need and lure, infinite being, the eternal now. This field of

Figure 2.1

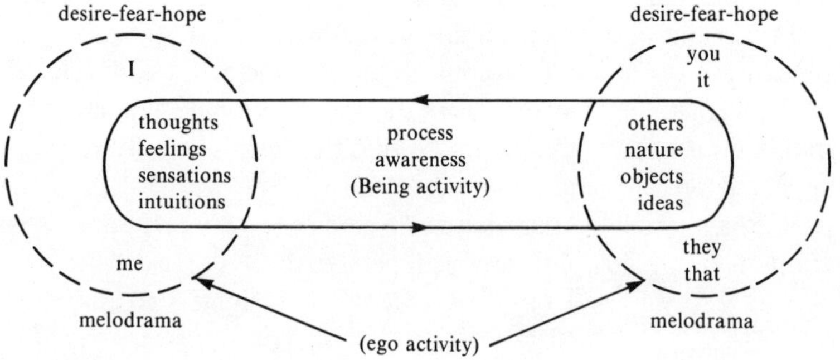

desire-fear-hope   desire-fear-hope

I   you
                                                           it

thoughts   process   others
feelings   awareness   nature
sensations   (Being activity)   objects
intuitions   ideas

                                                           they
me   that

melodrama   melodrama
                    (ego activity)

interacting life processes we shall refer to as *Being Activity*. Our knowledge of it will be referred to as *process-awareness*.

The dotted circles represent the world as we have learned to perceive it and have been acculturated into believing it to be. While there is pragmatic truth in this view of reality, it is only a partial truth, which is both its insufficiency and its illusional quality. This "objective" perspective is based on our experience of a finite existence that can be explained only through reason and our linguistic forms of differentiation and dichotomies. It is a world of separated forms, isolated existences. It is the basis of our constant efforts to manipulate, control, help, change, interfere with, dominate, disturb things in order to get what we think we do not already have: happiness, rooting, a sense of positive relatedness, some form of lasting continuity with life. And it is this very limited perspective of reality that results in the futility of all our efforts. We can only realize, not become, what we already are!

The term "ego" is being used at this point as it is used in many religious-philosophical writings, namely as a synonym for "self" or "I-process." In modern psychological writings, the term "ego" refers only to a portion of personality functioning—that which has to do with choosing, assessing, judging, directing behavior. We shall integrate the philosophical and psychological terminology in Chapter 6.

A finite perspective of a world of dichotomies is the basis for those psychotherapies that stress the understanding and strengthening of the ego. It is also the view of reality adhered to by those philosophies and religious interpretations that stress "will power" as the means to maturity. This perspective is illustrated in Figure 2-2.

Maturation, from this viewpoint, consists of opening up the channel "I" (ego, adult) and the inner world of subjective experiences so as to deal more effectively with the world "out there." It was Freud's basic faith and hope: Where there was id, let there be ego. TA's familiar "I'm OK—You're OK" comes from a similar notion of human fulfillment. What is critical about

Figure 2.2

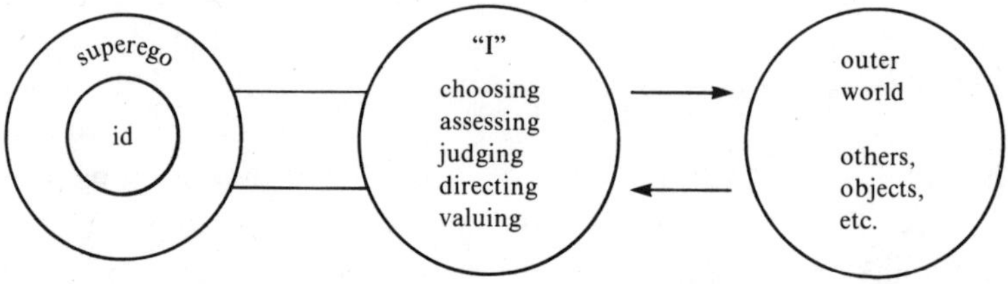

this perspective is the centrality of ego functioning for a satisfying individual identity. The insufficiency of this perspective is man's essential alienation from the rest of existence no matter how pleased he may be with his own autonomous functioning.

The alarming consideration that emerges is that the very effort to help people toward strengthened ego identity may itself be fostering a deep sense of alienation from life itself. If alienation is the primary cause of emotional disturbance, as the existentialists postulate, then such helping efforts become futile gestures. One may end up "happier" in his alienation, but fundamentally just as alienated as before he was "helped."

Both separative ego awareness and relational process awareness are common experiences for us all. Process awareness is commonly associated with peak experiences and may be dubbed "regression in service of the ego" or a "beautiful experience." On the other hand, process awareness may be seen as a revelation of the nature of reality, sometimes strikingly apparent, at other times dimly perceived. When process awareness is taken seriously it can lead to a shifted sense of identity. Let us explore some variations of this mode of experiencing.

Being Activity and Process Awareness

A commonly used term to describe the experience of Being activity is *egolessness*. This refers not to a stoppage of ego operations but rather to a sense of identity-centering that is beyond the scope of the ego's creation. Ego activities continue but are merely part of the total life process rather than its imagined center. Process awareness is the experience of Being activity and is commonly described as: identity with process, creative power, or love-generating acceptance.

Identity with process refers to the experience of actually being the total activity of all forms in a given situation. Sitting on a sunny hillside, one experiences being sun shining as much as skin being warmed, breathing as well as being breathed, green grass standing in curved sprouts and leg tickled by grass, wind blowing and hair moving. There is no sense of one thing causing another thing to happen. Everything is happening at once. The greenness of grass is as much a requirement of the makeup of the grass as it is of the sun shining and my eye seeing.[7] Such process identity is called "Satori" in Zen, a moment of enlightenment. Psychedelic drugs have generated a similar way of experiencing oneself as total process. Descriptions of this may be found in the drug experiments of Alan Watts, Aldous Huxley, and Carlos Castaneda.[8] Similar experiences, without the aid of drugs, are common among people who meditate and those who enjoy actively the beauties of nature.

An important aspect of this experience is the clear freedom from all ego attachments: fears, desires, passions, judgments, sentiments, alienation. Concerns about past, future, death, failure, success, are empty ideas of no consequence. Instead, one feels a profound sense of rooting in life as it is at this very moment. One is this totality of life going on as it is in all its complexity and apparent free play. There is an immense sense of tranquillity, which affirms everything as OK just being the way it all is. "I am that I am." In contrast to boredom at doing nothing of importance one experiences a heightened, energized state of aliveness, completeness, perfection. One's sense of time is lost as one steps momentarily into the eternal, the infinite. The religious person may describe this as sharing in the Divine Presence that permeates all things.

A most poignant description of identity with process is set forth in David Harding's book *On Having No Head:*

> What actually happened was something absurdly simple and un-
> spectacular: I stopped thinking. A peculiar quiet, an odd kind of
> alert limpness or numbness, came over me. Reason and imagina-
> tion and all mental chatter died down. For once, words really
> failed me. Past and future dropped away. I forgot who and what I
> was, my name, manhood, animalhood, all that could be called
> mine. It was as if I had been born that instant, brand new, mind-
> less, innocent of all memory. There existed only the Now, that
> present moment and what was clearly given in it. To look was
> enough. And what I found was khaki trouser legs terminating
> downwards in a pair of brown shoes, khaki sleeves terminating
> sideways in a pair of pink hands, and a khaki shirt front terminat-
> ing upwards in—absolutely nothing whatever! Certainly not in a
> head.
>
> It took me no time at all to notice that this nothing, this hole
> where a head should have been, was no ordinary vacancy, no mere
> nothing. On the contrary, it was very much occupied. It was a vast
> emptiness, vastly filled, a nothing that found room for everything,
> room for grass, leaves, trees, shadowy distant hills and far above
> them snow covered peaks like a row of angular clouds riding the
> blue sky. I had lost a head and gained a world.[9]

This description of process identity suggests an accompanying
ecstasy of beauty, unity, and total relation. Most of the time there
is no ecstasy accompanying such process identity. Zen masters
even warn students of the dangers of the joys that may occur in
moments of enlightenment. These pleasurable feelings can
quickly become a new bondage that will actually interfere with
seeing life for what it is.

"One's everyday life is the way," is a Zen directive. "When
hungry, I eat; when tired I sleep." The way is experienced in
simplicity, often in what would appear to be mundane activities.
"Have you finished your breakfast?" inquired the teacher. When
the student nodded, he received his most profound teaching for
the day: "Then go wash your bowl."

To identify with process does not necessarily mean one will be
experiencing all that happens about him as himself. Such experi-

ences, when they occur, tend to be momentary, intuitive flashes. The more common experience of identity with process results from a practice of awareness that accepts the individual ego as an activity, but does not take it seriously as some isolated identity. One allows oneself to be moved by a force other than the ego-control efforts. This may be referred to as the natural wisdom of the universe, no-mind, as it arises in one at any given moment. There is a certainty about what one must do next. There is a single, perfect action to be performed now. This could be a sneeze, the watering of a plant, or a snooze.

The ego will be involved in these activities, of course, as it works with the no-mind directional sense, but the ego will simply be viewed as part of the process: Earth in pot is dry—plant wants water—pitcher in cupboard—filling pitcher with water—pouring water on plant. Ego takes on evaluating and directing activities just as pitcher takes water-holding activity and water takes nourishing activity. Where is one's center? Nowhere! It all just happens.

The religious person may experience God as both need "within" and lure "out there." The experience of process-rooted identity is necessary in order to appreciate what finite existence is all about. Our being in touch with infinite experience places our finite ego-identity concerns in appropriate perspective, and it is this new vision of ourself in relation to the world that enables us to love.

This activity of love, of relation, is the fundamental force that permeates all of existence. The Christian may talk about meeting Christ in each person one encounters: "In so much as you have done it unto the least of these, my brethren, you have done it unto me." In each act of affirmation of the world, whether toward a friend or an enemy, a dog or a tree, a worm or a moth, a blade of grass or a rock, you are experiencing an inner affirmation at the same moment. "Grace is everywhere" is the dying declaration of Georges Bernanos's country priest.[10]

In addition to identity with process there is a different form of experiencing of Being activity called *creative power*. Poets and artists are familiar with this state of mind, and scientists, philosophers, artisans, and mechanics commonly share the same experience. Robert Pirsig describes the creative moment as "Quality" in *Zen and the Art of Motorcycle Maintenance*. He points out that, at the moment of Quality, subject and object are not differentiated; rather there is a complete identity of subject and object in the situation.[11] Nikolas Berdyaev describes these elements involved in the creative act: one's talents; that which is offered by the situation; and man's freedom. Freedom is an act of transcending one's usual sense of ego identity. Berdyaev's theology sees this as a call from the Divine (through one's gifts of talent and skill as well as the offering of a confronting situation) and man's response by actualizing his freedom through a temporary abandonment of all egotistical concerns.[12]

The creative moment is experienced as a temporary loss of self-preoccupation as one enters the unknown. This unknown is experienced as an excitement, as a pregnant moment about to deliver. That which is new can be discovered only in the unknown. An integrating process between the old and the new is occurring aside from any efforts to control or factor out such integrating efforts. There is the "aha!" and then some expressive act through the world of finite relationships. Berdyaev sees the creative moment as the primary process, and its expression, as in some art form, for instance, the secondary process.

Zen Buddhism has been allied with a variety of art forms: swordsmanship, archery, judo, Haiku poetry, Sumi brush painting, flower arrangement, and tea ceremony. Samurai warriors practiced Zen meditation in order to overcome fear of death and at the same time actualize their skills and power in moments of combat. The no-mind state of Zen is the same as Pirsig's "Quality."

In a discussion of Zen and swordsmanship, D. T. Suzuki described the no-mind experience as follows:

> But when the sword is held by the swordsman whose spiritual attainment is such that he holds it as though not holding it, it is identified with the man himself, it acquires a soul, it moves with all the subtleties which have been imbedded in him as a

swordsman. The man emptied of all thoughts, all emotions originating from fear, all sense of insecurity, all desire to win, is not conscious of using the sword; both man and sword turn into instruments in the hands, as it were, of the unconscious, and it is the unconscious that achieves wonders of creativity. It is here that sword play becomes an art.[13]

Carlos Castaneda describes his harried years as an apprentice to the Yaqui Indian sorcerer, Don Juan. In a recent book, *Tales of Power,* the test of this learning is his use of power. The power is exhibited in ways that defy our usual conceptions of how "reality" works—its usual laws defining time–space relationships. For example, we find Don Juan in two places at the same time, Mexico City and Sonara; we find Carlos and his friends leaping off cliffs yet being unharmed. Don Juan describes two different experiences of reality: the "tonal" and the "nagual." The tonal has to do with one's world of finite perceptions and meanings. The nagual is the source of power for everything within one's tonal. In order to avail oneself of the world of the nagual one must completely abandon all self-conceptions, worries, "inner chatterings." The nagual is bound by no rules of finite reality. It is the source of all creativity. The tonal can witness and assess but not create.[14]

Creativity, then, resembles identity with process in the act of ego transcendence. It differs insofar as process identity emphasizes appreciation of Being activity while creative power emphasizes an assertive engagement with this activity. Process identity is "knowledge of" while creative power is "use of."

The third way of experiencing Being activity is *love-generating acceptance.* In Christianity this is described as repentance and reconciliation through the grace of God. As we have seen, the experience of identity with process often occurs in moments of meditation, contemplation, and response to beauty. Creative power happens in relation to some life challenge that taps one's inner resources. Love-generating acceptance is a result of suffering.

The suffering involved here is perhaps the most painful of all suffering, and none of us are spared from such experiences. This is the suffering of one's bankrupt ego. One's efforts to be good, or mature, or loving, or courageous, or whatever, finally prove futile. One's autonomous efforts to find it, make it, keep it are inevitably in vain. One's hopes are eventually broken by the limits of life, whether this takes the form of error, ignorance, illness, accident, misunderstanding, or death. Paul Tillich describes these limits as the anxieties of fate and death, of emptiness and meaninglessness, of guilt and condemnation.[15] There are no havens of protection from these limits; and when we think there are, this too is an illusion that will in time be shattered: "I suffer therefore I am," was the recurring theme of Dostoevski.[16]

The act of repentance is actually the abandonment of some ego idolatry. One "loses one's old self," meaning a set of beliefs and hopes and maneuvers to secure happiness. Then, in this very moment of loss, of failure, of shame, of despair, one experiences a profound acceptance, an affirmation. Just when one feels of no value, he finds himself not only affirmed but, at the same moment, connected, rooted. Tillich describes this as "being grasped by the power of being."[17]

The Christian revelation is that Christ demonstrated by his life in history the meaning and actuality of this experience. Christ loved people of his time in spite of their sins—their prideful efforts, their fears and doubts, their foolish ideas. To view Christ as God in finite, human form enables some believers to understand the most important perspective about man's finite existence. God did not create this world as a testing ground for men to prove themselves—neither by good works nor endurance of suffering in order to make it into some other life thereafter. God created the world of finite forms so that the experience of love would be possible. Without a finite world there could be no love. Love takes many forms: care, compassion, conflict, creativity, appreciation, joy, grief, forgiveness. The point is that love requires more than one isolated being. It is an activity requiring dichotomies, differentiations. Through love one enters the kingdom of God while yet alive. The Christian commandment to love is useless as a requirement. No one can be ordered to love another. It becomes meaningful only when understood as a state of existence. This state may occur as a result of repentance. Having experienced grace, the acceptance and affirmation from God, one finds a similar love, forgiveness, caring generated spontaneously within oneself for the finite world of nature and other people. The fact that we fail again, as our re-emerging autonomous strivings encounter the limits of our finite existence, is no longer a despairing problem. For now suffering and repentance are our very means to a regeneration of love toward the world. Suffering is a gateway out of ego-isolation and into Being activity.

Love-generating acceptance results from humiliation. Humiliation has been described as seeing through every hope that is confronted by a limit of the world.[18] From humiliation emerges humility.

A common criticism of Christianity is that it either promotes self-righteousness or excuses a life of sin by guaranteeing forgiveness. When repentance is an existential experience, as described by Kierkegaard, Tillich, and Bultmann, it is the very opposite of either righteous pride or immoral maneuvering. Repentance is instead the defeat of ego strivings, the failure at control efforts. It is in the recognition of one's "unworthiness" that one's worthiness emerges.

Repentance is not only the province of Christians. The Jewish existentialist Martin Buber speaks of the same human activity as the "turning." It is a turning from an experience of the world from the "I-it" perspective, where all forms are objects to be manipulated, to the "I-Thou" perspective, where every experience offers the opportunity for relation. The Hassidic idea of "the hallowing of each day" is much like the Zen emphasis upon "every-moment-Zen" and like Christ's comparison of men with the flowers and birds who live in the present without worry over the future. This relation, this presence, is itself process-awareness. Martin Buber's description of "the meeting" (in the movement from "I-it" to that of "I-Thou") conveys a notion of love-generating acceptance similar to Christian grace: "In the moment of supreme meeting, Man receives revelation, but this revelation is neither experience nor knowledge. It is "a presence as power" which transforms him into a different being from what he was when he entered the meeting."[19]

Love-generating acceptance is an ego-transcending experience just as we saw in process identity and creative power. Identity with process emphasized appreciation and knowledge of Being activity; creative power had to do with active engagements and use of it; love-generating acceptance stems from personal disillusionment and results in an affirming rooting in Being activity. These three forms of process awareness are ways of experiencing Being activity through a quieting of ego preoccupation. They are really three ways of talking about the same activity: the realization of one's identity in the life process termed Being activity. At the very moment one experiences identity with the entire process of Being activity, alienation is overcome. The most critical human need—the longing for meaningful relation, connection, rooting—is fulfilled.

It becomes apparent that the solitary unhooks himself from some of the concerns of the other social work types that result in such professional bugaboos as paternalism, dogmatism, intellectualism, and utopianism. The solitary does this through an altered perspective about the nature of his own identity. Realization of this perspective is no small task, however, since modern Western society is geared to a fostering of ego identity and hence alienation. In the next chapter we shall see how the action of ego identity impedes the essential need for process-rootedness, or meaningful relations.

Notes

1. Sam Keen, "Sorcerer's Apprentice," *Psychology Today,* Dec. 1972.

2. Paul Reps, *Zen Flesh, Zen Bones* (New York: Anchor Books, 1968), p. 7.

3. Herman Hesse, *Siddhartha* (New York: New Directions Books, 1957), pp. 133, 145.

4. Zen Tale, source unknown.

5. R. H. Blyth, *Zen in English Literature and Oriental Classics* (New York: E. P. Dutton, 1960), p. 103.

6. Fyodor Dostoevski, *The Brothers Karamozov* (New York: Random House, 1950), p. 384.

7. This mode of experiencing is described in Alan Watts, *The Book* (New York: Collier Books, 1967), Chapter IV, pp. 80-100.

8. Alan Watts, *The Joyous Cosmology* (New York: Vintage Books), R. S. de Ropp, *Drugs and the Mind* (New York: Grove Press, 1960), Aldous Huxley, *The Doors of Perception, and Heaven and Hell* (New York: Harper & Row, 1963).

9. D. E. Harding, *On Having No Head* (New York: Perennial Library, 1972), p. 6.

10. Georges Bernanos, *The Diary of a Country Priest* (New York: Image Books, 1954), p. 232.

11. Robert Pirsig, *Zen and the Art of Motorcycle Maintenance* (New York: Bantam Books, 1975), p. 234

12. Nicholas Berdyaev, *The Destiny of Man* (New York: Harper Torchbooks, 1955), pp. 126-32.

13. Daisetz T. Suzuki, *Zen and Japanese Culture* (Princeton, N.J.: Princeton University Press, 1970), p. 146.

14. Carlos Castaneda, *Tales of Power* (New York: Simon & Schuster, 1974), pp. 118-46.

15. Paul Tillich, *The Courage to Be* (New Haven, Conn.: Yale University Press, 1952), pp. 40-63.

16. Laszlo Vatai, *Man and His Tragic Life* (New York: Philosophical Library, 1954), p. 95.

17. Tillich, *Courage to Be,* p. 173.

18. Vatai, *Man and His Tragic Life,* pp. 94-110.

19. Maurice S. Friedman, *Martin Buber: The Life of Dialogue* (New York: Harper Brothers, 1960), p. 75.

Chapter 3

Ego as I-Process

Being activity may be considered a natural rhythmic process that is ongoing and operative within all men. It can be characterized as responsive, ever changing, emerging, and maintaining a constant relation between one's sense of individual unique personhood and the world through which one moves. Its functioning is both integrative and creative. These two activities of Being are a constant interaction between the psyche's relation to itself (biological, psychological, and spiritual components) and its world of people, nature, material objects, and ideas. At any point in space and time Being activity is the relation between what is unique in the person (emerging needs, potentials, limitations) and what the momentary situation calls forth from him. For this to occur in a meaningful, human way requires the cooperation of ego consciousness. Being activity may be said to be the total psyche–environment interactive process as experienced by the individual person.

The ego's activity is essentially a paradox. As I have said, Being is the active process of the psyche–environment interaction. There is no separation of the "I" from the world. The existential term "being-in-the-world" expresses this unity, connectedness, relation. Yet in order to exist as a human being one must differentiate oneself from others. Ego is the conscious, cognitive expression of the creative–integrative core of Being activity. This cognitive expression takes the form of making meaning

out of experiences. Man must have a past and a future; an awareness of death and of his own limitations; a notion of who he is,
where he wants to go, how he should relate to others, and what he
should do with the opportunities presented to him in points of
space/time. The paradox of the ego, according to existentialism,
is that the ego achieves maturity, enlightenment, final satisfaction
when it realizes that its task of differentiation was just that—a
task—which had its usefulness, but that in fact the individual and
his universe are not separate entities at all but a single meaningful
process.

The existentialist emphasizes the choosing ego, the individual's awareness of freedom, of divining his own purpose, of being
a no-thingness—being other than a thing in itself, as Sartre's
Being-for-itself. The existentialist refuses all identities, roles,
"oughts" put upon him by family, society, and tradition. Truth is
subjectivity, says Kierkegaard.[1]

But if there are no absolutes, rules, guidelines, truths, then on
what basis does the ego make its choices? This is the abyss the
existentialist faces as he confronts an "absurd universe." If the
universe is absurd it can provide no answers. Various existentialists offer different and sometimes contradictory responses to
this question. The resonse is always made in inwardness, by an
affirmation of one's subjective experience. Yet this inwardness
may be egotistical and even demoniac—potentially destructive of
self and others—or it may be fulfilling and life affirming.

The pained central character in Dostoevski's *Notes From Underground* demonstrates the demoniac. While this man know-
ingly chooses to act in ways that are self-destructive, his very
actions are experienced by him as a positive rebellion against the
conforming expectations of others. His allegience is solely to the
completely free expression of any unconscious whim or impulse,
whether self-defeating or not. Even while so "possessed" he
feels more alive as a human being than he would in robot-like
subservience to standards defined for him by outside authorities.

Another response to the abyss is to live with the "absurd" as
something given and unresolvable. Here there may be some hope

for life as possibly meaningful, but without any known entry by which man can experience and know this meaning. No choice can be the ''right'' or ''relational'' one. This perspective is that of the lost characters of Franz Kafka and the ''waiting tramps'' of Samuel Beckett.[2] Here the ego's ability to choose is of little value except insofar as one can resist roles and definitions thrust upon him from outside himself.

Then there is the ''authentic man'' who draws up his own code on the basis of the values he derives from his life experiences. One thinks of Sartre, Camus, and Hemingway as men who defined how they would live in order to fulfill themselves as individuals and to imprint their world view upon others. While one remains individual in an alienated world, one has a sense of dignity in holding to what he believes to be true for himself and feels a relationship of compassion with others who are in the same predicament of isolation and knowledge of coming death. The ego's freedom and task of meaning-creation are the essential part of personality for the authentic man. The unconscious is as much an absurd abyss as is the outer world, and he holds to his own conscious direction-giving power for his sense of meaning. This image resembles the perspective of the psychoanalyst, who sees man's hope in the ego's autonomous power to consider the forces of a capricious id, a superego, and outer environment and make a personally satisfying choice.

In all three of these examples, man remains trapped within his alienated ego. This is the pessimistic core of much modern existential literature. The critical question is whether this is the inevitable noble and courageous stance that is left for us in the face of life's realities, or whether such ego entrapment may itself be a form of self-deception.

In our model of identity through process awareness, man's ego is no longer such a central preoccupation. If ego-identity is a stark and desperate clinging to man's last and final hope, then process-identity becomes even more radical a stance; for here one lets go of even the ego and plunges into the chaotic unknown. As we shall see in the next chapter, such a plunge can have its dangers.

What happens when we view the ego, or self, as essentially a figment of the imagination, a nonentity, a false identity? Zen Buddhism and Krishnamurti share similar views of the illusional quality of the ego.

The birth of the "I-Process" (ego) occurs early in life as a result of the natural process of differentiating oneself from one's surroundings. This process is necessary for survival—to be able to maneuver in the world. Since the purpose of "I-Process" is survival, its corollary—loss of or failure to develop individual identity—is experienced as potential death. From very early in life, then, the need for an "I-Process" is believed to be of life-and-death importance. Considerable anxiety and dread are stirred up when one's individual identity is threatened. Throughout one's life the prospect of certain death at some unknown moment in the future is always a potential limit that threatens to wipe out one's earned identity. Similarly, such experiences as pain, doubt, meaninglessness, and guilt threaten the integrity of one's identity. So one binding force of the "I-Process" is fear.

In contrast to these painful, threatening experiences there are pleasurable experiences that the "I-Process" wishes to repeat or hang onto as long as possible. These may have to do with the instinctual gratifications or the pride that comes from achievements and appreciation by others for living up to an identity that one has believed to be right, good, and true. Desire becomes the second binding force of the "I-Process." Desire (and its companion, hope) results in ongoing efforts aimed at repeating pleasurable, reassuring experiences that rejustify one's identity.

The "I-Process" itself is nothing more than memory. Even when the thinking process integrates new meanings (resulting from very recent experiences) with existing memories, these new meanings are themselves already memories of some recent experience (even as recent as a minute ago). What gives the series of memories the illusion of being an individual identity is one's continuity of thought. One keeps the thought process in motion by judging, evaluating, worrying, regretting, pondering, and desiring. Don Juan called this "the internal dialogue."[3] Even our efforts to put linguistic labels on our feelings and sensations, to name them, is a method of maintaining "I-Process" continuity. Our integration of memories with one another is our most convincing experience of being a self with historical autonomy.

In reality there is no personal self. There is a series of memories interspersed with moments of inner silence as well as with moments of creative realization (emerging meanings). Similar to thoughts are sensations, feelings, and intuitions that arise and disappear. It is helpful to understand this process as a series of separate items strung together so as to appear continuous.

Let us imagine a woman sitting home alone one afternoon. She *feels* lonely; has a *memory* of an old boyfriend; then a *memory* of a love scene she saw on television the day before; then the *thought* of turning on the television set now and tune in on the same show; then the *sensation* of excitement as she moves from her chair toward the set. If you asked her what had occured she would say, "I was lonely, so I turned on the TV." Her sense of autonomy and identity continuity would be secure. What makes this thought process, driven by fear and desire and maintained by continuity, so convincingly an "I" is the undergirding belief that what is happening is affecting and being affected by an onlooking observer called "me." Loneliness was happening to *me*, so *I* did something. Without that center, "I," loneliness would be simply an arising emotion. If this emotion were looked at in the same way as leaves trembling on a tree limb as the wind blows, there might be an altogether different sequence of events. As we shall see in a later chapter, change occurs by altering the way one experiences that which is happening.

The "I-Process" results from an interplay of freedom and mechanistic determinism. In existentialism, unlike psychoanalytic and learning theory, man is not perceived as victimized by his unconscious. He is not automatically molded by his environment. Man's freedom of choice is not a result of a nurturing early childhood. His potential for choice is ever present, regardless of age, regardless of traumatic childhood experiences, despite dehumanizing and oppressive social environments. Man is a victim only of his own mind.

As already indicated, even as an infant, he creates his own meanings about what is happening to him in his effort to differentiate himself from his surroundings. True, his choices or opportunities for doing something about it may be exceedingly limited, but this does not change the fact that he is always the creator of his own meaning of experiences.

It is not long before he has collected a memory bank of images that define himself and his world according to positive and negative judgments he has made. These "good" and "bad" images are connected with roles in which he has found himself: child, student, friend, adolescent, worker, spouse, parent, church member, tennis player, and so forth. It is this memory bank that operates in a totally deterministic manner whenever he experiences himself as "I-Process."[4]

The woman experiencing loneliness as something happening *to her* immediately taps into the array of self-images that results in her conclusions about the meaning of this troubling feeling and tells her what she must do about it. Personal melodramas (basic life scripts, catastrophic expectations) are always the result of self-created images and supporting beliefs about why, etc.

Man's "first and last freedom," as Krishnamurti puts it, is to experience his "I-Process" for what it is. One loses the I-as-victim experience the moment he sees thoughts as thoughts, feelings as feelings, just as he sees birds as birds, clouds as clouds. Since he is the one in charge of his experiencing, it is his use of his own awareness that either perpetuates the "I-Process" or moves beyond it into Being activity as process awareness. In our earlier evaluation of process awareness (identity with process, creative power, love-generating acceptance), we found that each experience of Being activity was accompanied by a sense of self-transcendence. It is this activity of transcending the ego that Krishnamurti refers to as freedom.[5] Determinism characterizes the ego of "I-Process." Freedom, creativity, and experiencing the new occur only as one enters the unknown. What is known is already past memory. What is uniquely new must therefore be in the realm of the unknown.

If process awareness is ever available to us, then why do we refuse or ignore it? Because the ego consciousness, the "I-Process," is a most formidable, relentless opponent. We dearly love our ego consciousness and delight in the notion that it is a separate creation of our own whose development we carefully guide. We therefore cling to whatever encourages this "I-Process"—thoughts, feelings, prejudices, desires, habits. It is not only pride but also fear that tempts us to the enhancement of the ego. The fear of loss of the sense of ego-identity is much like the fear of death. Without this "I-Process" as the heart of our operation there is a fear of nothingness, of void. It is this continuing effort to enhance our own ego that results in persistent restlessness and craving.

Actually we prefer the agitation of being aware and concerned about "I-Process," for this heightens our sense of being. The alternative, the natural state of personality, is stillness, quietness, emptiness, nothingness. There is a lack of the sense of "I" in a calm silence that merely responds to what occurs. This immobility is feared, for it represents a lack of self, a void. We prefer reassurance of our existence. Unfortunately, the very existence we seek to preserve is a finite one, defined by finite relationships and activities. It is therefore inevitably the cause of our continuing anxiety, for in being related solely to the finite we are grounded in insecurity and fear of death.

Christian existential writers, like Kierkegaard and Dostoevski, present man's "I-Process" dilemma in different language, but their perspective is remarkably close to the thinking of Zen and Krishnamurti. Laszlo Vatai, writing on Dostoevski, defines the tragic as man's longing for the infinite while bound by the limits of his finite existence.[6] This is another way of describing man's basic need for transcendence of the entrapping, alienating "I-Process" so as to enter an experience of fundamental rooting in relation. He must be a part of what is other than himself. This need has been described as his longing for immortality.

The entrapment of the ego is experienced as alienation, of being adrift in a world of isolated forms. Both Kierkegaard and Dostoevski described three escape routes commonly used to handle this human dilemma. These are conformity, passion, and rationalism.

Conformity, the preoccupation of current American novelists and playwrights, is the subjection of one's identity to an identity set forth and affirmed by others. Here is the "mass man" of Kierkegaard. Dostoevski's "underground man" was willing to endure shame, misery, and self-castigation rather than offer himself to others as a conforming automaton. Conformity is an artificial effort to root oneself in life's process. It is not life that one becomes rooted in, however, but rather the fickle agreements and judgments others have made about life. Paradoxically, the more one conforms to the expectations of others, the farther one is from one's own subjectivity. And it is only through one's subjectivity, one's personal experiencing or awareness, that one can ever be with the flow and vitality of life as it actually occurs.

Passion, on the other hand, is man's most vitalized effort at escaping alienation. The pursuit of intense states of emotion and sensation allows one, at least momentarily, a sense of freedom and connection. Here is Kierkegaard's "aesthetic man." Vatai describes passion as a means of trying to sweep aside all limits. In such moments the nightmare of death and a life of suffering are forgotten. Passion is the greatest mover of life, Vatai points out, and it moves man toward the transcendent. Through passion man vividly encounters the limits of life. In his subsequent disillusionment man may become a knower and lover of life. Passion broken upon the limits of reality and responded to with wisdom can dissolve into compassion. But passion may also become a futile, endless cycle. Passion narrows and restricts at the very moment it intensifies. No sooner have the fires died down than they must again be rekindled in order to find another pacifying moment out there.[7]

The third escape route is rationalism—the elevation and idolization of reason. This is man's effort to define for himself some matter of importance, some ultimate concern, to which he can devote his efforts and bring about satisfaction or happiness in some future moment. Here is Kierkegaard's "ethical man."

Projects of reason may take the forms of scientific pursuits, philosophizing, social reform, professional competency, or defining a personal code to which one seeks to adhere. Vatai points out that the danger of reason lies in its creation of dogmas with which it opposes life. The intellectual tends to relate to other men through his ideas, not directly. The rigidity of dogmas cannot accept the vitality of other possibilities, and therefore fear and suppression are nurtured.[8] In rationalism man substitutes some future achievement, or some present effort of organized control, for direct relation with the flow of life process. This flow is too threatening, for it appears to the rational mind as chaotic, ungoverned, senseless. Here was Freud's fear of the id that necessitated his championing the ego.

Each of the three escape routes will in time be disrupted by the limits set forth by life. When this occurs one encounters a choice. One can revolt against the limits, either by pursuing his old escape route with enhanced vigor or by choosing some other escape route. The other alternative is to resign the ego before the limits by accepting the tragic basis of human existence and affirming a faith in the meaningful mystery one comes upon in his moment of ego transcendence.

The perspective developed thus far has presented a view of man's possibility for maturation through process awareness of Being activity. This effort alone frees him from the variety of entrapments he creates for himself by ego-security operations. Although a religious perspective has been helpful in describing process awareness, one need not utilize religious symbols in order to understand it. Zen writers sometimes resort to religious symbols and at other times do not. Krishnamurti avoids such references.

The basic life philosophies that at present affect the social and psychological sciences should not be differentiated on a religious/nonreligious basis. A more accurate description would be process-rooted/ego-rooted positions.

If one does not see man as rooted outside his own ego, then one necessarily must remain with a basic ego position: Man is autonomous and makes his way through this world essentially alone. He deals with this alienation in one of two ways. (1) He may seek to improve human relationships through control of society and/or through his efforts with other people in his everyday life (family, neighbors, fellow workers). This is the hope of overcoming alienation by creating a world of caring and affirming human relationships. (2) Or, in the humanistic existential view, he believes such efforts at human control to be largely futile, and so he accepts man's basic alienation and derives his sense of meaning and integrity from being true to this perspective of the human condition. Dignity stems from taking responsibility for the meanings he makes and activates in a universe that is otherwise alien and uncaring.

The humanistic existentialists are closer to the process-rooted group than are those humanists who hope for eventual happiness through improved social institutions and human relations. The humanistic existentialist does feel a bond with all human beings: It is in his keen sense of compassion for man's essential aloneness and his wish for a meaningful connection with a disinterested universe. But this love is different from a love generated by a fundamental acceptance and experience of relation. The love of a humanistic existentialist is a kind of desperate outreach, a mutual pity, a shared nobility.

The ego-rooted group might criticize the process-rooted perspective by declaring the very idea of Being activity to be a deception of the ego, nothing more than wish-fulfillment, as Freud pointed out. The process-rooted believer would have a similar reaction toward the ego-rooted position. He would see such insistence upon man's fundamental ego isolation as itself an example of the ego's primary illusion. A belief in absolute individual autonomy is essentially a rebellion of the prideful ego against the limits encountered by life. There is a fundamental refusal to allow for the possibility that its existence may be grounded in something other than itself. For if this were true, the ego would have to sacrifice its precious notion of its own control of its destiny, happiness, and salvation. If the process-rooted perspective is seen as a wish to return to the womb, the ego-rooted perspective would be viewed as refusal to give up one's adolescent rebellion.

We have here two opposing faiths. There may be no proof of the rightness of either perspective except as an individual commits his own life to one of them and lives it through, seeing how it comes out. But even then he is proving his perspective only to himself. Until recently the mental-health professions have tended to ally their theory and practice with the ego-rooted position. It is time that the alternate possibility had its hearing.

Fortunately, the split between ego-rooted and process-rooted identities need not be an either/or choice. Christian theology handled this split through the concept of the Trinity. Castaneda dealt with it by affirming both the tonal and the nagual modes of experiencing. Zen does not separate a clear affirmation of individual forms from the common reality called Buddha Nature. I shall deal further with this issue in Chapter 5.

Notes

1. Kurt F. Reinhardt, *The Existentialist Revolt* (New York: Frederick Ungar Publishing Co., 1960), Chapter 2 (Kierkegaard), pp. 23–58, and Chapter 5 (Sartre), pp. 156–76.
2. Eugene B. Borowitz, *A Layman's Introduction to Religious Existentialism* (New York: Delta Books, 1966), p. 221.
3. Carlos Castaneda, *Tales of Power* (New York: Simon & Schuster, 1974), p. 233.
4. Robert Powell, *Zen and Reality* (New York: Viking Press, 1975).
5. J. Krishnamurti, *The Flight of the Eagle* (New York: Harper & Row, 1971), pp. 8–22.
6. Laszlo Vatai, *Man and His Tragic Life* (New York: Philosophical Library, 1954), pp. 58–79.
7. *Ibid.*
8. *Ibid.*, pp. 79–93.

Chapter 4

States of Mind

We have seen how the solitary re-evaluates his own identity through an exploration of reality as he experiences it. His own search for meaning, through personal engagement with his own subjectivity as it interacts with the field of life process before him, results in an affirmation of the highly unique, individualized world view of each human being. No categories can fully explain him, no system of thought fully define him. Each of us creates his own reality, and the most we can do is seek to understand the special, private world views of others. Each person is his own diagnostic category.

Being activity was described in Chapter 2 as including both outer (environmental) and inner (subjective) components. We saw how interpretations of inner experience could lead toward either process-identity or ego-identity. Chapter 3 explored the inner forces that tend to attach us exclusively to an ego identity. In this chapter we shall see how one moves from an inner experience to the construction of a world view and related value system. This is of central importance in existential thinking, for the most valued aspect of a person is his self-chosen world view—the meanings or purpose that propels him. Without absolute, legalistic outside guidelines, the individual is left with his own inner constructs, for which he is held solely responsible. We shall also find that the kinds of subjective experience that result in the construction of varied world views are basically shared by all people. It is the interpretation given to these experiences that results in conflicting world views. World views are ego-identity constructs and lend themselves to alienation and superiority/ inferiority judgments.

Four states of mind are universal in human experiences and are the experiential foundations for varied identities and associated philosophical world views. Each of them is experienced, on occassion, by all of us. We tend to find ourself in one state most of the time and the other three for either fleeting moments or more prolonged periods. When we experience any state of mind, this affects our entire view of the world. Our values may begin to shift along with our interests and energy level in accord with the mental state of immediate awareness.

Panic-Apathy-Rage. This is the extreme of negative experiences: horror, dread, hatred, rage, anguish. The world seems chaotic. One is a helpless cork bobbing upon an absurd sea of painful waves or else boring calm. One feels totally checkmated; there are no apparent moves left. One's hopes have been devastated by a clear vision of their emptiness, their utter futility. One may wish to strike back against this painful, apparently senseless world, or one may feel completely immobilized. One will often feel on the edge of an abyss—perhaps of death, perhaps of some unknown other world. There may be a sense of being totally possessed by alien forces that seem bent upon destruction, and one believes his soul to be lost. Those who are dominated by this mental state have been described as psychotics and psychopaths. If there were TA terminology to do this state justice the label might be "It's not OK," which is a conclusion not about only oneself and others but about the entire universe.

Security Image. Here we have a state of mind that has been described by psychological theories in terms of defenses, life script, topdog/underdog splits, dysfunctional reinforcement system, catastrophic expectations, irrational beliefs, unworkable values. This is the home of the neurotics, the character disorders, and most other diagnostic nomenclature. The world view here, in TA jargon, includes: "I'm OK—You're not OK," "I'm Not

OK—You're OK,'' and ''I'm Not OK—You're Not OK.'' One does not necessarily have neurotic symptoms, however. The existentialist would describe mass man, or people in ''bad faith,'' as living out of this category. What most clearly defines the security-image state of mind is some specific image that one identifies with and believes is somehow fixed within one's personality. Such images will vary according to the situation, as one has a storehouse full of them. Images will be both positive and negative. We experience them in the subjective process of ongoing, rigid self-evaluation and judgment: good husband in that occurrence; bad father in that occurrence, etc. This is an egotistical (self-idolization) process that interferes with letting our attention move beyond ourselves. We can drive home from work without noticing anything around us because of our preoccupation with self-praise or self-blame, our worries or regrets. Most of us reside in this mental state a good share of the time. The primary concern of the Security Image is protection—to survive. This is Martin Buber's world of I-it.[1]

Pragmatic Self. Here is our usual model of emotional maturity: the self-actualizing person who knows and effectively uses his potentials; the integrated ego that has disposed of irrational defense systems and has appropriately sublimated drives; one who is clear about his own identity and integrates this effectively with the many roles he plays—parent, worker, spouse, friend, and so forth. His identity allows for flexibility, for change. Here is TA's ''I'm OK—You're OK'' stance. One lives in a world of priorities, responsibilities, opportunities, projects, values, expectations, logical cause-effect relationships. Planning, organizing, evaluating, and analyzing are predominant activities. Matters of consequence hold our attention. Judgment, in this state of mind, is not related to egotistical concerns of pride and blame but rather to pragmatic results: does it work?

No-mind. This is a state of mind that moves one to an experience of synthesis beyond dichotomies. One may feel an identity with the total process of forms and activities occurring within his awareness. One experiences transcendence of his usual sense of separateness. This may come as a unifying experience with another person, with the world of ideas, with nature, or in the rhythms of music, dance, or a sport activity. One may feel rooted in a Divine power beyond himself, like the mystic. One may share vitally in the experience of another person, or all of humanity, as sometimes occurs with the actor, the comic, the empathetic psychotherapist. One may experience a direct, personal relation with nature, as does the primitive hunter or farmer. Children, poets, idiots, and old people with wisdom will tell you of the no-mind world in different ways. Here is Buber's world of relation: I—Thou. If TA had a category for this experience of life, it might be "It's OK," meaning the totality of one's immediate awareness.

In order to evaluate how these mental states are often related to one another let us examine Figure 4-1. Several implications may

Figure 4.1

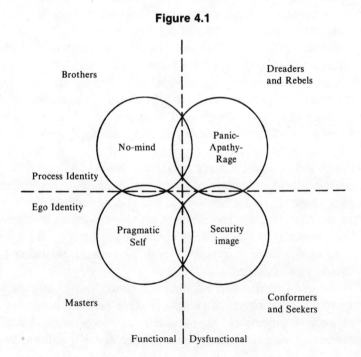

be drawn from this line of thought:

1. Although all people experience all four states of mind at times, individuals tend to act as if only one state were the "true" one for themselves. They tend to identify themselves with a particular mental state and organize their lives (world view) around this identification. I have labeled the character life styles associated with each state: the dreaders and rebels of life; the conformers and seekers of life; the masters of life; and the brothers of life.

2. When the four circles are divided horizontally, we find that the no-mind and panic-apathy-rage mental states are similar in their process-identity experience of life. These are functional and dysfunctional expressions of the similar experience of "egolessness" or nondifferentiation. Similarly, the pragmatic self and security image states are both centered upon a clear sense of self-identity, the former functional, the latter dysfunctional.

3. When we divide the circles vertically we find that no-mind and pragmatic self are both examples of functionality. The panic-apathy-rage and security image states represent distortions of life experience and are dysfunctional in various ways.

4. The position of the circles suggests a set of interrelationships between the mental states that would appear generally true, although there are exceptions. Each state is most strongly influenced by the two states that overlap it. This is not to say that the other, the fourth state, is not experienced too, but it tends to be a less influencial factor.

The panic-apathy-rage state can sometimes move into the realm of no-mind, and at other times in the direction of security-image activity. Its greatest deficiency is in the pragmatic-self state (no solid, positive sense of self-identity). This is obvious with psychotics and to a large degree, as we shall see, with psychopaths.

The security-image state is commonly experienced as conflict, between the hope of pragmatic self-realization and the fear of panic-apathy-rage "disintegration," or loss of control and identity. Ambivalence between these very hopes and fears characterizes this state. No-mind experiences are often seen as threatening to the control of the security image and are therefore avoided.

The pragmatic-self state has a flow into and out of both no-mind and security-image states. But the master of life is so secure in his realistic sense of identity that he seldom experiences the panic-apathy-rage states.

The no-mind state will sometimes lapse into the pragmatic self and at other times into panic-apathy-rage (i.e., psychotic breaks, suicides, and violence, sometimes seen among novelists and graphic artists). However, the no-mind state is most alienated from the security image, for it sees the security-image state as a clear illusion.

Diagnostic classifications place people on a continuum of mental health–mental illness. Certain categories are closer to the "illness" end (psychotics and psychopaths). The model suggested here is an effort to move away from the value judgments associated with diagnostic categorization. We shall see that certain assumptions about those most "seriously disturbed" may be erroneous. Assumptions we have made pertaining to id, ego, and superego functioning in relation to diagnostic types affect our attitudes and prognoses toward people so diagnosed.

Underlying efforts of helping professionals to promote "mental health" while attacking and altering "mental illness" stem from an assumption about society that subordinates the individual to the "good of society." Control over the lives of people through the institutions of society (courts, prisons, schools, welfare departments, psychiatric hospitals becomes the mode of realizing this goal of social improvement. Who decides what the good society is to look like? The very people who are being invested with more and more power to change it. These sociologists, social workers, psychologists, psychiatrists, and others by and large hold to an ego-rooted perspective that defines how man should function.

As we look more closely at the dreaders and rebels, the conformers and seekers, the brothers and masters, we may see some of the complexities of evaluating the "goodness or badness" of people's functioning.

Conformers, Seekers, and Masters

People living primarily out of security-image experiencing often manage to be happy. They commonly achieve a sense of patterned regularity or tradition in their lives. They may surround themselves with friends who validate the more important positive perceptions they have of themselves. "I'm just this way" is their self-comforting and stabilizing message to the world. They will also arrange their activities and use of time so as to provide them with reassuring feedback. This is why unstructured time periods, as on Sundays, holidays, or during vacations, are commonly threatening experiences. The security of the self-image is nurtured by a denial of responsibility for certain areas of their lives—they usually provide justifications and excuses to explain why they behave and think as they do. There is a kind of self-validation in this deterministic perception of themselves. They often excuse others from being responsible just as they do themselves. This is not to suggest a lack of discipline. They may be rigidly dogmatic about how they must behave, and these behavioral rules define the essential images that are so precious to them.

The happiness of the conformer or seeker is not always a result of living up to his security image. It is not uncommon for such people to allow themselves experiences of a no-mind quality without attaching any special significance to these experiences other than that they are pleasurable or relaxing. Fishing, sailing, dancing, playing musical instruments, sports, hiking, even "tinkering" with minor fix-it jobs around the house, all are common activities in the lives of these people. If they were to examine the potential meaning of such experiences (does this mean there is a different way of understanding reality?) they might either retreat quickly in fright or dismiss such notions as irrelevant.

The conformer and the seeker differ from the master of life primarily in their vulnerability. There is a rigidity about the identity image they hold that can be disrupted easily by the vicissitudes or flux of life experience. The master of life has a clear sense of identity with a flexibility that allows for change and reassessment without undermining his sense of being a self of value.

Another distinction is in the degree of narcissism, or egotistical control, connected with their identity sense. The concept of narcissism is used here to mean a centering upon self to such a degree that all other aspects of existence are of secondary importance except as one may use them to prove his basic rightness or, better, righteousness. The more one is insecure about his identity, the more rigidly one must control his life experiences—including his own feelings as well as other people. The master of life can live out a life style of need satisfaction and fulfillment of abilities almost as if engaged in a game. There is an essential satisfaction in being himself as a response to a variety of life situations, whether positive or negative feelings result, for his sense of self is secure. The conformers and seekers must ever seek reassurance of their security, which requires control efforts.

As mentioned, conformers and seekers may lead lives that are relatively happy. The price they often must pay for this, however, is energy spent in suppression of emotion and/or manipulative control of others. Behind the suppression of emotion is the self-splitting ambivalence that tears at their very pillars of a secured identity. This ambivalence can be so painful that it threatens them quickly with identity confusion. This torturous ambivalence is dramatically illustrated by Raskolnikov in Dostoevski's *Crime and Punishment* as well as by Bob Slocum in Joseph Heller's *Something Happened*.[2] These characters reveal the painful conflicts that surface when control efforts are insufficient.

Slocum is a model of the modern existential antihero. Heroics result from commitments, and commitments necessitate some basic faith and direction. When absurdity predominates, one's identity can shift precariously with one's mood or free associative rambling. Behind the mask of security-image experiencing is this absurd antihero in us all. The slogan of our day: So what?

A common hypocrisy of today's helping professional is his failure to see himself as trapped in absurdity, no less than his client is. His efforts to distinguish pathology from "healthy functioning" are often vain attempts to reassure himself that he really is something that he is not. Most of us are rooted in security-image values and idolize this manner of experiencing. Our diagnostic categorizations are efforts to subdivide the broad security-image operation so that we may see others as more neurotic than ourselves.

Dreaders, Rebels, and Brothers

Recent writings about psychotics and psychopaths suggest the peculiar notion that they may be closer to saints than those of us with an ordinary degree of social and personal adjustment. R. D. Laing sees psychosis as a functional effort to break out of de-humanizing, restrictive social and family relationships.[3] Norman Mailer almost two decades ago recommended psychopathy as the most effective means of releasing human energy and potential in an otherwise conforming, security-conscious society.[4] Our psychological theories essentially have supported our prejudicial attitudes toward those who threaten us most—the psychotics and psychopaths. Rather than condemn them as evil and possessed, we have condemned them to having very weak egos, unworkable superegos, and almost no hopeful prognosis for response to psychotherapy. Our treatment efforts have been aimed at helping them "adjust" in order to form workable security images, and these efforts have largely been in vain.

On the other hand, artists, novelists, playwrights, film makers, and the general public have been increasingly fascinated by the worlds of psychotics and psychopaths. What attracts us about these types? Why are many of the most popular actors and actresses characteristically associated with psychopathic roles? Perhaps we are attracted to these life styles because they live out something that we value and wish we could live out ourselves.

In an attempt to remain consistent with our psychologies, we have explained this fascination by saying that we are an overcontrolled and repressed society, and so our impulses for sex and violence are allowed expression only through identification with characters in television, films, and novels. But this is too simple an explanation, and highly questionable. We are far from the repressed society of which Freud was a part in Vienna at the turn of the century. Could it be that we are attracted to the psychotic and the psychopath because of a secret realization that they are more genuinely human in certain respects than ourselves? Both the dreaders and the rebels of life have this in common with mystics, Zen masters, and other brothers of life: They are disillusioned with the hopes for security and happiness that dominate the rest of us. The world of finite realities is an absurdity. There is no way to achieve happiness by trying to manage and control such a world.

What is it that the psychotic experiences in his hallucinations and delusions? Is it a distortion of reality through a projection of his fears and wishes? Are his psychotic experiences self-created and therefore an immense self-deception? Or is the psychotic penetrating the usual curtain of everyday reality and actually experiencing a different level or realm of reality, like Castaneda's strange "separate reality" of experiences with drugs or in nature without drugs, or the mystic's experience of the totality of his life as vibrant, responsive, interactive, meaningful exchanges of profound significance, or the clairvoyant's world of telepathic communications and astral projections?

Sensory-deprivation experiments performed with normal people resulted in psychotic experiences.[5] Here psychotic experience had nothing to do with a deprived childhood or a poorly functioning ego. It had to do with the simple, straightforward experience of being deprived of any sense of relation to something beyond oneself. There was nothing to be responsive to or interact with in any meaningful way. The ego had to experience relation beyond itself. Perhaps at the point of sheer desperation, the ego sees that which it has learned not to see: its essential connection to life beyond itself. This experience may take a variety of forms: the virgin Mary, a green-eyed elf, a talking coyote, or the voice of a dead spouse. But the experience itself may be one of relation, not projection, and therefore meaningful. What form a person gives to this experience might depend upon his cultural training and belief system. Where "talking to God" is a common description and explanation for certain experiences, then it is more comfortable to have conversations in which one actually hears God talking.

There are two frequently reported experiences associated with psychosis. There is the "happy" psychotic who is at peace with his psychosis and prefers it to the world of "reality" to which others would have him adjust. Then there is the psychotic who suffers keenly from his psychotic experience—sometimes in panic, sometimes in utter despondency, sometimes in rage.

The "happy" psychotic may be experiencing a most meaningful sense of connectedness with life through his pcyhosis. He does not want to be disturbed by those who say he must play the game another way, by finding relation through a pragmatically effective self-identity that behaves "realistically" in dealing with the world. Who is to say that the happy "psychotic" has not moved from his psychosis into a realm of meaningful, no-mind experience? Is his talking to the birds and the trees any different from the experiences of St. Francis of Assisi?

The suffering psychotic may be in pain for various reasons. First, his pain may be caused by those who are important to him but who reject him as "crazy" as long as he achieves his sense of meaningful relation to the universe in ways they do not understand. He feels torn between allegiance to his own meaningful sense of relation through psychosis and his wish to maintain a positive relationship with significant others. Laing points out that this type of pain is exacerbated for patients when the entire hospital staff and his therapist join his significant others and seek to "get him well."[6]

Another possible source of the psychotic's pain may lie in his own interpretation of the psychotic experience itself. If the experience is a revealing relational contact with another realm of reality, it is still left to the individual to interpret the meaning of that experience for himself. If he believes that this new experience is a chaotic crumbling of all he has known before, he may well experience panic. If he interprets it as "forces" pursuing him out of hostility, his reaction might be hostility or fright. If he interprets the experience as some controlling fate, he may feel hopelessly despondent. Since the psychotic person has a poor sense of his own identity, in most cases he can be expected to interpret such experiences in a negative way. The very fact that he usually comes from a disturbed family life makes it likely that he will project parental expectations onto this new force or presence, resulting in fear, anger, suspicion, and confusion. It is important to note that we are not talking about the psychotic experience as a projection but, rather, the meaning attached to it.

On the other hand, this weak sense of ego identity can also be productive. The psychotic can see through the façade of self-deceptions, false hopes, and empty control and achievement efforts, and laugh at that whole world of people wrapped up in their own matters of serious consequence. The happy psychotic often has seen this absurdity and therefore can dismiss the efforts of helping professionals to readjust him to such a state of confused games and deceptions.

A twenty-five-year-old woman was referred to me by another therapist because she wanted to talk only to a therapist who was acquainted with Zen. She had been diagnosed a schizophrenic even as a child and had been in and out of institutions all her life. Now she was married and had two children. She had returned to college on a part-time basis and had become emotionally attached to a professor who was frightened of her overtures. When he clearly rejected her advances, she began to experience psychotic phenomena again. She represented a mixture of the happy and panicky psychotic. On the one hand, she believed there was validity to her view of the world. She saw most people, including staffs of hospitals and a series of previous therapists, as involved in ego "games" that she perceived as futile and empty. A brilliant person, she had read everything written on schizophrenia and had rejected much of it as erroneous. In Zen literature she had discovered the concept of no-mind and the illusion of the ego. These made sense to her in her experience of the world. Instead of feeling ashamed of never having developed an effectively socialized ego, she had begun to believe that she might be ahead of the socialized masses in this respect. She wanted a therapist who could also see such value in her personality.

What panicked her, however, were her delusions of being the cause of destructive occurrences in the world, like car accidents and plane crashes. She was also preoccupied with the professor who had rebuffed her and had some vengeful fantasies about him.

If we talked of her everyday concerns—family, marriage, school—she quickly lost interest. Zen was our common reference point. I agreed with many of her conclusions about the shortcomings of an ego-dominated society. I also accepted the similarities she pointed out between Zen's "Suchness,"or no-mind, and the state of stunted ego development describing schizophrenia. Some of her childlike behavior was reminiscent of that of wandering Zen monks. In the course of these talks I mentioned to her the concept of "makyo" as a means of getting some perspective on her frightening delusions. "Makyo" is the variety of strange, often frightening phenomena experienced by people who meditate for extensive periods of time. Zen masters reassure students that they should look upon such hallucinatory phenomena in the same way as any other occurrences in meditation: simply observing them without judgment or attachment. I recommended she read a book on Zen that described this occurrence (Kapleau's *The Three Pillars of Zen*[7]), which she did. She experienced enormous relief, and within days the frightening delusions had subsided.

What this example illustrates is that psychotic phenomena may be preserved in a negative fashion by the fear associated with them. Once the fear is altered by a shifted perspective and the phenomenon is simply accepted without concern, both the fear and the delusion are very likely to go away. The same thing may occur for the "happy" psychotic. He holds on to his phenomenon out of pleasure rather than fear. It may be unfair to call the woman described above as a "happy psychotic," for her happiness resides not in the psychotic phenomena itself but in the way she has come to view herself and others as a result of insights about ego functioning and game playing derived from her life experience, which included psychosis.

The fact that the psychotic may let go of his psychotic experience does not in the least invalidate the experience itself. This is the same situation described in the previous chapter in relation to forms of process awareness. While process awareness may be accompanied by ecstasy, as in moments of meditative unity, heights of creative insight, and immersion in love-generating grace, these experiences are not lasting. They are welcome and revealing but must not be taken as ends in themselves. In Zen, one can let go of such experiences so as to live his mundane, everyday life as the way.

One more approach to understanding the pain of the psychotic person is based on the manner in which psychosis occurs. One usually does not feel that he has chosen to experience psychotic phenomena, as a meditator chooses to experience no-mind or a clairvoyent chooses to experience psychic phenomena. The psychotic, rather, feels suddenly "possessed" by powers or forces he does not understand and has not invited. Even when Carlos Castaneda chose to participate in some drug experiment under the guidance of Don Juan, he has still at times terrified by these experiences. He even contemplated hospitalization and suicide. Similar happenings have resulted from psychedelic drug experimentation among young people.

The area of overlap between the no-mind and panic-apathy-rage states is a hopeful concept, on the one hand, but a risky concept on the other. Don Juan warned of the dangers of "nagual" involvement (similar to no-mind) without having first developed a clear, strong tonal (similar to pragmatic self).[8] There are numerous examples of artists, novelists, and philosophers who have crossed this overlapping area from no-mind into panic-apathy-rage with resulting suicide or psychotic breakdowns. Robert Pirsig in *Zen and the Art of Motorcycle Maintenance* presents a vivid description of this position as he walks the tightrope between the two states.[9]

There is an effort in Laing's writings to romanticize the psychotic's experience.[10] The appeal here is to young people, particularly those who are part of the drug culture, for their very hope is to experience life by getting beyond the social expectations, restrictions, and entrapments of everyday existence. "Blowing one's mind" has a connotation of self-induced insanity.

Interestingly enough, when some of these no-mind-seekers sought to make a saint of Carlos Castaneda he quickly rebuffed them. In his extensive apprenticeship with Don Juan he learned of the pain, anguish, discipline, and ongoing struggle of the spiritual quest. Through Don Juan's guidance Carlos could see the difference between the terror of insanity and the power of "seeing" (enlightenment).

Katsuki Sekida, writing on Zen training, clearly differentiates between psychosis and the Zen enlightenment experience. While he sees similarities among the psychotic's experience, the "aura" of the epileptic experience, LSD perceptions, and the Zen Enlightenment experience, Sekida emphasizes a critical difference. This distinction has to do with the sound operation of the pragmatic self (as we have called it) in conjunction with the no-mind experience. There is not a melting away and loss of the sense of the separative self; rather, the enlightenment experience involves a clear awareness of individual identity and process identity at one and the same time.[11]

Both Castaneda and Sekida seem to be emphasizing the same point. Enlightenment does not result from no-mind experiencing in and of itself. There needs to be, first of all, a clear and solid appreciation of one's own individuality and an affirmation of this personal identity within the wider context of process awareness. This is not unlike the emphasis in Judeo-Christian thought on acceptance of oneself and appreciation and care for others as essential for any meaningful mystical experience that links one with a broader reality.

It is one thing to appreciate the validity of some of the psychotic's experience. It is quite another matter to celebrate his experience and even seek it for oneself as some direct entry into enlightenment. Quite to the contrary, the psychotic may be open to aspects of reality that are more difficult for others to come by; however, he must still contend with the confusion and torture of his struggles regarding his individual identity and relationships with other people. His psychotic experience may open up new possibilities and even provide some hopeful directions, but the route of the psychotic's search is simply another form of individual striving toward understanding, with its own unique pains and sufferings. Such experiences may be appreciated but hardly envied.

There are some interesting implications here for the treatment of the psychotic. An important challenge for the therapist is to discover a way of validating the psychotic person through the psychosis itself, rather than imply that the patient is sick and will not be well until he gives up his psychotic process. This joining with the psychotic's world view is sometimes possible when his disenchantments with life have an element of truth for the therapist.

If the "happy" psychotic is really quite satisfied with his psychotic process, then the therapist may want to help him make the bridge between living with his psychotic process and living with the everyday world of family and work. "I'll be interested to hear what you and God talk about in the days ahead, but if you tell your boss you may be in the same old trouble." This is socializing a psychotic at his level of truth—helping him play games in a game-playing world so as not to distrub what is far more real for him—the psychotic experience itself. This approach can also help many panicked psychotics move toward a "happy" psychotic state (which might sometimes be a no-mind state). With the "happy" psychotic we need not feel impelled to move him either toward enlightenment or toward society's standards of social adjustment. From one standpoint he may seem far from maturity, contentment, and happiness. But is he any worse off than many conformers and seekers whose lives remain dominated by ambivalence, compulsions, addictions, bigotry, and greed? They too live on with their pet distortions.

Laing suggests that those who have previously been psychotic and have been able to make a satisfactory nonpsychotic adjustment to life may be the best people to help other psychotics. There is a similarity here to the self-help philosophy popular in work among alcoholics and drug addicts. When psychosis can be viewed as a frightening yet enlightening experience, perhaps more people will be able to pass through it instead of retreating from it to please their families and therapists.

The psychopath represents an experience of the panic-apathy-rage state of mind far different from the psychotic's. He is commonly described as totally narcissistic, manipulative, without conscience (no guilt or sense of responsibility), restlessly on the move for excitement, without deep caring feelings toward others.[12] The psychopath shares with the psychotic the experience of disillusionment with the world of security-image strivings. While not experiencing psychotic activity, he lives in a state that might be likened to Don Juan's "death awareness." He is totally without hope. One cannot be loved, so there is no point in trying. One is of no inherent value, and there is no way to become valued. From this position of cynical egolessness, the psychopath is remarkably similar to the existential authentic man or the Zen man.[13]

He sees through all the game-playing and self-deceptions of the "serious" world of conformers and seekers. He has no wish to be like that. Instead of moving into a world of psychosis, however, he becomes an expert manipulator—outplaying the conformers and seekers at their own games. He uses trust without trusting, love without loving. When he acts in a caring, human way, like

Ken Kesey's McMurphy, he is doing so because it happens to provide him with some excitement and rebellious satisfaction.[14] Like the Samurai warrior, he is extremely alert and wary of his surroundings. He is highly invested in the moment at hand, rather than past or future, for that is where excitement is. Excitement is his only meaning. He is detached from any commitments to others that might obligate him to a particular course of action. He will do what feels right at the time. He has settled for a life of pleasurable satisfaction as often as possible. Without an inner sense of self-care and without outside relationships that convey this to him, he must seek meaning through ongoing actions that make something pleasurable happen. The psychotic disowns the world of everyday reality; the psychopath disowns the world of law, social expectations, and man's struggle through history for positive meaning.

The psychopath's similarities to the Zen and existential perspectives are these: freedom from outside authorities by finding truth in subjectivity; disillusionment with the worldly hopes of conformers and seekers; commitment to alertness in the moment at hand; experience of personal nothingness, egolessness; a semblance of discipline and effort for doing what he does well; emotional detachment from the game efforts of others. He views life as a perpetual game, not building toward anything, but simply going round and round; and he projects a charisma that attracts others.

The linkage of saint and psychopath has been explored in literature, notably in the fiction of Jean Genêt and Henry Miller, in Dostoevski's exploration of "underground man" and Raskolnikov.[15] Camus's *The Stranger* is a character whose behavior puzzles the reader—is he paychopath or authentic existential man?

In *The Pornography of Power*, Lionel Robinoff points out that Mailer and Genêt express a common concern about the polarity of creation and destruction.[16] It is only as man is able to penetrate his own hypocrisy and face honestly the evil within himself that there is any hope for his rebirth in creative growth. The psychopath lives out this evil in his life style. Mailer sees such a handling of evil as qualitatively different from confessing evil thoughts to an understanding therapist. To *be* one's evil results in humiliation and realization for rebirth. To *understand* one's evil intellectually is often simply another way of excusing it and avoiding humiliation. Robinoff points out that one can experience his own evil in the imagination, rather than having to commit evil acts. He sees that Genêt's purpose as playwright is the portrayal of evil in its own right, without excuse or justification. This art form can provide the reader or theatergoer with an imaginative realization of his own evil through an identification with characters portrayed. As long as we deny our own evil by projecting it onto others or rationalizing it away we are in bondage to our own hypocrisy, and growth is restricted.

What the psychopath represents here is a daring, unflinching honesty of evil intent. He does not delude himself with the excuses and justifications that shore up the security image of the conformers and seekers. The psychopath often appears fearless in his actions, and this is because he has nothing to lose. He is already dead to hopes of happiness and security. He experiences much of his own aggression as a striking back at a hypocritical world that is essentially uncaring and two-faced. He will play the world's game of using and controlling others, and he will do it without hypocrisy, by the use of deception and by taking responsibility for his deceptive intentions.

To make a hero of a psychopath, however, is to indulge our aggressive fantasies. Despite Sartre's effort to portray Genêt as an evil-doing martyr, one cannot but wonder if there is more cynical pleasure than martyrdom in Genêt's exposure of the hypocrisy of his times.[17] While the psychopath may represent a daring and somewhat piercing self-honesty, he also represents a restricted form of human existence. His rooting in death awareness (death of ego hopes) has not resulted in a reconciliation with life as affirmation but remains a belief that all of life—all possible realities—is finally absurd, and therefore one might just as well use the world selfishly, to seize his own pleasurable satisfactions as often as possible. He is fundamentally an autonomous rebel who screens out experiences of human compassion, warmth, and caring from his base perspective of what he is willing to accept as true. His own brand of bad faith is in refusing any validity to life-affirming experiences. In this respect he remains more influenced by the security-image state of mind than the psychotic despite his overall rejection of the hopes and pursuits common to most of us. He fears that hurt may result from any kind of trust. He is trapped by his own self-chosen boundaries, which define affirming experiences (through impulsive satisfaction) and screen out the validating processes of life outside himself. He remains in a state of anxiety in his efforts to control life so as to give himself what he wants. He cannot trust life to be a teacher from whom he might learn. The sufferings of others are their own concern. Each person looks out only for himself. When he suffers it only feeds his underlying rage and cynicism. Vengeance and rebellion are his home base.

What of our treatment of psychopaths? First of all, attempts of therapists to adjust and socialize them to a more responsible life style would be just as futile as they are with psychotics. Such efforts are based upon a perspective of life that the psychopath, in all self-honesty, must reject. His own knowledge of the games and the deceptions of conformers and seekers is often more realistic and profound than that of the therapist who works with him.

Like the psychotic, the psychopath needs to be validated within his own framework of psychopathy. His basic honesty, daring, and disillusionment are valid points for such affirmation. From this base of understanding, it may sometimes be helpful to point out how his chosen life style is hampering his attainment of what he wants. If he is in jail his freedom of activity is seriously impaired. This is another version of trying to socialize a psychopath without requiring him to accept a different conclusion about life or happiness.

A more basic change, however, has to do with enabling the psychopath to experience some positive sense of relatedness to other human beings. This may be almost impossible for the therapist or priest to accomplish, for his own life style represents a philosophy alien to the psychopath's experience. The psychopath would view such efforts as brainwashing. But to hear such life-affirming ideas from one of his own kind could make a marked difference.

The experience of Malcolm X may reveal a valid direction for treatment. His criminal life in the ghetto before his imprisonment represents a psychopathic life style. What resulted in his conversion to a responsible, caring leader in the black movement? His contact with Black Muslims while in prison seemed to result in this remarkable change. The Muslims reached Malcolm X through his hatred—the same hatred shared by the Muslims for the white world. A sense of compassionate, caring allegiance was born in Malcolm X for his fellow suffering black brothers and sisters. While this conversion was born in hatred, Malcolm X later transcended it, breaking with the Muslims to establish his own group. The break was in part a result of Malcolm's affirming the idea that not all whites were devils. One might speculate that the psychopath can be reached most directly through his hatred, but if such human experiences as compassion and allegiance and responsibility are generated in him, other positive human emotions may be released as well—such as a broad capacity to trust and care.

It may seem unfair to label an outstanding leader, such as Malcolm X, a psychopath. However, both Alan Harrington and Mailer suggest a broad meaning of the psychopathic concept. This is not a clinical description of a weak ego and malfunctioning superego;[18] we are talking of a basic attitude toward life. Mailer pointed out that most ghetto blacks have no need for the disillusionment the existentialist poses for middle-class white society; the life of the ghetto has been one of disillusionment from the start. When one experiences the world as hostile and depriving and sees the apparent security and happiness of the majority of society as unavailable for oneself, one lives out a perspective of alienation and disillusionment akin to psychopathy.

Ingredients for change for Malcolm X included a realization of his self-defeating life style based on reports of others who had shared it. This is not unlike self-help groups such as Alcoholics

Anonymous and Synanon. The new element, however, was an affirmation of Malcolm's disillusionment within a framework of hatred for white society and the use of this very force as a vehicle for commitment to a new life style, which included a concern for others.

How these ingredients might be incorporated into treatment programs for psychopaths is a creative challenge for the helping profession. One thing seems clear, however, and that is that our usual socialization efforts, which invariably involve the teaching of middle-class values (those of the conformers and the seekers), are a waste of time for the true psychopath.

Why is it that so much literature has dealt with the "failures" of life: the psychopaths, addicts, psychotics, alcoholics, tramps, criminals? It is because these people have all shared a common human experience—humiliation, the bankruptcy of the ego, the shattering of those very illusional hopes still dominating most of us. From this standpoint these "failures" are closer to some realities of human existence than are those of us who are still securely socialized.

As helping professionals we have failed with the "failures" through our efforts to debunk their insights and to brainwash them into socialization. When state-controlled departments of mental health link their funding of institutions and clinics with statistics indicating success according to prescribed standards of socialization, we see how powerful the forces of social control can become. Helping professionals become the keepers of minds, the architects of family and community living.

Rather than continue to tyrannize the psychotics and psychopaths, we may find that the most effective way of inviting positive change for such people is a stance that accepts and validates them within their own life perspectives. When one is provided with room to conform his existence to his own experience, and realizes that it is understood and even validated to some extent by others, there is greater likelihood of change. The surest means of entrenching psychosis or psychopathy is to fight with it or force its suppression through drugs or other socialization pressures. Suppression is seldom an enduring life stance. We have handled the recidivism of psychotics and psychopaths by blaming deteriorating egos and insufficient superegos, not our own distorted views of pathology and social values.

We have seen in this chapter how conformers and seekers, dreaders and rebels must be appreciated within the perspective of their own dysfunctioning. Without basic respect and the willingness to wait and let be, the helping professional can expect therapy to be a game of power struggle and stubborn resistance or else deceptive subsurvience. To affirm the validity in dysfunctional behavior is not to disclaim the value of having some model of functional behavior. The lure of what is possible for man is as important a motivation for change as is the pain of his self-deceptions and futile games.

The terms "functional" and "dysfunctional," like "healthy" and "sick," imply some value determination. To have an ideal model of human functioning is essential to us not only as helping professionals but as human beings attempting to find some meaning for our own lives. Value issues regarding religion, philosophy, and ethical decisions will be brought to us by our clients; these should not be dodged. The danger arises when we judge certain life styles as "bad" and seek to force others to comply with our idea of health and functionality.

Considering the states of mind described, we can look once again at the life-style perspective of the solitary. Rooted in process-identity, he seeks an interplay of the masters and brothers of life stances while at the same time accepting and respecting the stances of the dreaders and rebels, as well as of the conformers and seekers, that inevitably arise within himself. Chapter 5 explores this mode of life.

Notes

1. Maurice S. Friedman, *Martin Buber: The Life of Dialogue* (New York: Harper & Brothers, 1960), pp. 62–69.
2. Feodor Dostoevski, *Crime and Punishment* (New York: W. W.

Norton, 1964), and Joseph Heller, *Something Happened* (New York: Ballantine Books, 1976).

3. R. D. Laing, *The Politics of Experience* (Baltimore: Penguin, 1967), pp. 131–45.

4. Norman Mailer, "The White Negro," *Advertisements for Myself* (New York: Signet Books, 1960), pp. 302–21.

5. John Zubek, ed., *Sensory Deprivation: Fifteen Years of Research,* Marvin Zuckerman, "Hallucinations, Reported Sensations, and Images" (New York: Meredith Corp., 1969), pp. 85–125.

6. R. D. Laing, *The Politics of Experience* (Baltimore: Penguin, 1967), Chap. 5.

7. Philip Kapleau, *The Three Pillars of Zen: Teaching, Practice and Enlightenment* (New York: Harper & Row, 1966), p. 38.

8. Carlos Castaneda, *Tales of Power* (New York: Simon & Schuster, 1974), pp. 147–62.

9. Robert Pirsig, *Zen and the Art of Motorcycle Maintenance* (New York: Bantam Books, 1974).

10. Peter Sedgwick, "R. D. Laing: Self, Sympton and Society" in Robert Boyers and Robert Orrill, eds., *R. D. Laing and Anti-Psychiatry* (New York: Harper & Row, 1971), p. 37.

11. Katsuki, Sekida, *Zen Training, Methods and Philosophy* (New York: Weatherhill, 1975), pp. 179–82.

12. Alan Harrington, *Psychopaths* (New York: Touchstone Books, 1972), p. 38.

13. Ibid., 203–71, and Mailer, "White Negro," pp. 302–21.

14. Ken Kesey, *One Flew over the Cuckoo's Nest* (New York: Viking Press, 1962).

15. Harrington, *Psychopaths,* pp. 24–48.

16. Lionel Robinoff, *The Pornography of Power* (New York: Ballantine Books, 1969), p. 199.

17. Jean-Paul Sartre, *Saint Genet: Actor and Martyr* (New York: Braziller, 1963).

18. Harrington, *Psychopaths,* p. 198.

Chapter 5

The Pragmatic-Self/No-Mind Interplay

The master of life may exhibit a variety of life styles. He differs from the conformer and seeker in that his life style is not primarily an effort to maintain some fixed image for his own sense of security and worth. His identity is fundamentally secure, and this allows for a flexibility in his living. He no longer needs to prove his adequacy and goodness by his control of feelings, behavior, or other people.

Some purposes commonly realized in the life styles of the master of life are establishing love relationships and making them last; ongoing efforts for social and political reform; a responsible effectiveness in ordering and living out family, social, and professional roles; accomplishing specific tasks or goals often related to creative satisfaction, the achievement of power, or the sotution of problems.

To the extent that the master of life is rooted in his pragmatic self and ignores or dismisses the importance of his own no-mind experiences, he pursues these purposes as matters of serious consequence. He views himself as an autonomous individual in a world of other individuals and life forms. Loneliness, isolation, and alienation often accompany a strong sense of autonomy. The autonomous person is rooted within finite existence and is therefore maintained by desires, hopes, and fears that have to do with the needs of others as much as his own.

In contrast to this, the brother of life experiences himself as being rooted in the infinite, the transcendent, much of the time. And when he is not, he is seeking a rerooting there. To the extent that he ignores the importance of his own pragmatic self, the brother of life will become immersed in no-mind experiences that seem to ignore the problems of the everyday world of himself and others. As a mystic, he may be interested only in the life of prayer or in the maintenance of some "nirvana-like" experience. As an artist or a musician, he finds life meaningful only when he is in the selfless heights of creative activity. There are also peak-experience hunters who organize their lives around such possibilities. These may take the form of sensuality, excitement laden physical activities, and experimentation with psychedelic drugs. Somewhat related are those whose ventures take the form of habitual oblivion, addicts of alcohol, drugs and gambling. At this point it becomes increasingly difficult to distinguish the no-mind state from the panic–apathy–rage state of mind. There is often a strong tendency to view oneself as omnipotent, and this may take the form of seeking and developing psychic powers. While the brother of life may experience a profound rootedness in the transcendent, in the unity of all existence, he will at the same time be alienated from the everyday problems of his fellow human beings except when they become students, followers, or fellow mystics, artists, and sensualists, sharing and reassuring one another about the validity of their life style.

There is an alternative to the master or brother position. This is the process-rooted identity described in Chapter 2. In this perspective all four states of mind are appreciated and validated as expressions of life process (the way life is at any given moment). Yet one's own identity as a separate individual (a centered self, an ego entity) is altered. One is no more attached to the no-mind state than to the pragmatic-self state. One tends to live in the interplay between pragmatic-self and no-mind states, but this does not completely exclude the negative counterparts of these states, the security-image and panic-apathy-rage states.

In Figure 5-1 the security-image state is represented by the

Figure 5.1

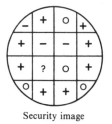 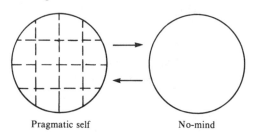

Security image   Pragmatic self   No-mind

gridiron system of dichotomous thinking, which becomes the alienating overlay between our perceptions and our direct experience at any given moment. By rigid beliefs, related to both long-standing and recent shifting patterns of judgment, the mind classifies reality into positives (+), negatives (−), and neutrals (0). There may be occasional unknowns (?), but these are reduced as much as possible by the prejudicial control the mind maintains over what is allowed into awareness. The security-image mental state is commonly experienced as matters of consequence, catastrophic expectations, and control necessities (both of others and of one's own feelings).

This way of diagramming the security-image state also includes the panic-apathy-rage state of mind. The only difference is that for the dreaders and rebels most of the identity classifications are more uncertain, more tenuous. Such doubts and uncertainties about self and others result in the psychotic's occasional shift in and out of the world of conformers and seekers. The psychopath, as we have noted, does have one fixed certainty—his mistrust of the world and his related hostility. He is able to utilize the gridiron system of the conformers and seekers in a way that the psychotic cannot. The psychopath learns this grid so as to manuever effectively to get what he wants, but he does not take these judgments and stereotypes of reality seriously.

The functional model of pragmatic-self/no-mind interplay is illustrated differently. In this process-identity model we see that in the pragmatic-self mental state there remains a dichotomizing process of categorizing reality. The dotted lines, however, represent a flexible (rather than rigid) use of beliefs, judgments, meanings. The existentialist describes this as the realization of the world of dichotomies as absurd, which is different from meaningless. Castaneda labels this perspective the "world of folly," yet maintains the need of a strong tonal (pragmatic self) in order to engage such a world for the joys, sorrows, creative opportunities it can provide.[1]

The zest of living requires engagement with the desires, passions, pleasures, fears, and pains that life affords us. Yet we need not take our grid system so seriously. Here we have Jesus's "being in this world but not of this world" and Kierkegaard's "absolute respect for the absolute telos and relative respect for the relative telos."[2] Here, too, is the similarity between saint and psychopath—a sort of games-as-games perspective on the world of dichotomies. One may commit and invest oneself in any undertaking, but the meaning does not lie in its successful outcome. It is the creative, caring, appreciating, playing, suffering process itself that is meaningful. To live in responsive relation to the flow of life is sufficient. Awareness, alertness, and willingness to risk whatever identity one is currently playing out characterizes this pragmatic-self state.

What differentiates the pragmatic-self/no-mind model from the psychopath is the recognition of and meaning given to the no-mind state of experience. There is a flow between pragmatic-self and no-mind awareness that will happen spontaneously when security-image preoccupations are not interfering. This is experienced much like the figure–ground process in Gestalt psychology. Those ambiguous pictures in Gestalt-perception studies of vase and faces, or of old witch and lovely young woman, illustrate the flow experience.[3] One sees the picture in one way at one moment and in quite another way at the next moment. One is in the pragmatic self's world of dichotomies and then suddenly in the no-mind state of wonder, emptiness, nondichotomy. Just as suddenly, the perception of reality may shift back. For the psychopath, the no-mind experience is simply another exciting satisfaction. For the master-brother of life the no-mind illumines the absolute telos, the firm rooting in life as affirming process.

The no-mind state is revealing of reality as process-rooting, yet it is not a prized state of tranquillity or ecstasy to be sought as often as possible. What the no-mind state reveals is that life is perfect just the way it is—without any judgement or security effort to maintain an individual identity. One experiences a silence, a "point of no abode," a center of immobility that is untouched by ego concerns and security-image fears and longings. Thoughts, feeling, sensations come and go like clouds shading the sun. When it rains the ground gets wet. When it grows cold one puts on warm clothes. Life is the way it is. There is a natural perfection here that can be understood only intuitively. This is not an irrational cop-out but rather a way of understanding one's experience through means other than the reasoning intellect. Does one require some reasonable purpose to appreciate a flower blooming or the sun shining? The flower blooms; the sun shines!

There is no controlling ego center that must be protected and judged and constantly evaluated. The mind is memory, the accumulation of thoughts. It operates in a completely mechanical fashion. Although one chooses the meanings of arising situations, these choices are in reality the effect of meanings one has concluded over a period of many years. What was once a free choice of meaning has now become an automatic process of attaching meaning to triggering situations. Yet one remains responsible both for the original creation of the meanings and for maintaining the automatic process.

Similarly, one does not choose what he must do in any given situation: There is a process of organism-environment interplay that clarifies one's realistic need or potential for action, provided that one does not interfere with this natural process. Even when the ego assesses when and how some emerging need will be dealt with, the ego is being directed creatively from within, out of natural wisdom.

There is in reality only one choice open to us—Krishnamurti's "first and last freedom." This is the choice of how we experience a given moment. We can do this from either the ego-rooted identity or the process-rooted identity. From the process-rooted identity we are detached from and yet accepting of our memories, anticipations, judgments, regrets, desires, fears, confusion. They come and go as stars come out at night and as leaves fall from a tree.

Our way of experiencing can be affected as much by the pragmatic self as by the security-image or panic-apathy-rage states of mind. We go on a picnic and it rains. Why is that a problem? Who is it that is troubled by such an occurrence? Life process is as much planning and going on a picnic as it is the gathering of clouds and the rain falling. To experience oneself as responsible for the rain as much as for the picnic is to undercut the problem. But one gets wet! Yes, one does. To be troubled about getting wet and one's picnic plans going awry is also life process being itself. But when one experiences the entire range of happenings in this process-identity framework one is detached from the usual rage, despair, and guilt about things not going "my" way. One is free from the usual melodrama that preoccupies us.

This interplay of pragmatic self and no-mind results in a life style of humility and rootedness. It is characterized by an intensified sense of presence, of availability to whatever arises. And it is this very movement of life process that supplies one's sense of identity through a rootedness, a connectedness. In this rootedness is a sense of power as well as completion. Life is perfect as it is. One's energy is freed from controlling efforts—there is nothing that *must* be different. One's activity is a responsiveness to whatever arises, and this takes the forms of caring, compassion, creativity, and appreciation. Such activity itself has a profound effect upon the world through which one moves. Love is no longer a strained effort—it simply occurs. One does not love; he is in a state of loving. "I am that I am." It's OK!

The master's-brother's stance fully affirms and accepts the activities of both security-image and panic-apathy-rage states of mind within himself. While the pragmatic self's use of alert awareness as well as of the games-as-games perspective often acts as a shield to the seductive and forceful efforts of the security-image and panic-apathy-rage impingements, there will be times when one is successfully hooked by those states of mind. There will even be times when he will intentionally hook himself as a momentary protective effort. Once hooked, for whatever reason, there are varied ways of returning to the pragmatic-self/ no-mind interaction state.

This "unhooking" process might be termed disillusionment or humiliation. It is the process of rendering impotent whatever image (and accompanying judgments) has become of central and dominating importance. On occasion insight about one's past patterns is sufficient to manage this. More often, the disillusioning process is effectively handled only by direct engagement with life process, as experienced.

Engagement aimed at disillusionment can occur both subjectively and interpersonally. The subjective action is simply heightened awareness of the inner painful or craving process, as we see in Gestalt techniques, in Krishnamurti's "observation," and in est's method of sourcing (assuming full responsibility for the cause of one's experience).[4] By "letting it be," by giving full attention to one's inner process, one frequently finds that it will soon change.

When such subjective efforts fail it is usually because one is also caught up in some interpersonal game, where his troubled state is being reinforced by others and where the subjective state itself is an effort to manipulate or control others. If this is true, the humiliation process must include interactions with others.

Interpersonal humiliation may occur in three ways: intensification of games, or control maneuvers; alterations of interpersonal transaction patterns; and life style shifts. The intensification of games, repetitive problematic interactions with significant others, is simply a matter of doing more of the same. If the conflict is about competitive arguing, then compete and fight all the more strongly. In order for humiliation to occur, one must actually hope for exposure of his own part in the game. Exaggeration will often reveal the absurdity of a position otherwise effectively justified.

Changing transaction patterns is a kind of experimental play, when one is unsure about the game in which he is stuck. If impulsive arguments are the issue, for example, then one might try controlled arguments, only allowing them at prescribed times. The goal here is not to stumble upon the right solution, but rather to shift the habit patterns, which in turn will usually affect change in one's attitudes and feeling responses. Once these changes begin one may soon realize the purpose served by the game and new options will open up through this exposure.

The final means of "unhooking" from an interpersonal bind is a life style shift, which is the most drastic and risky: a job change, a marital separation, abstinence from alcohol or smoking, a change of friends, each will provide the impetus for new experiences which may disrupt binding interpersonal patterns. As noted above, the very alteration of such patterns may prove sufficient to open one's awareness to new insights, and the accompanying disillusionment with former attitudes. One may, for example, realize that the previously imagined solution to the problem (a new job or companion) was in fact an illusion. With that matter clarified, one allows into consideration new possibilities.

Whatever the forms of humiliation, whether subjective or interpersonal of life style, the "success" of personal disillusionment results in an experience of reconciliation, of completion, of wholeness wherein the pragmatic-self/no-mind interplay is regenerated.

The description of a "functional," "healthy," "mature" model of personality is a very mixed blessing. Whether it is Freud's freed-up ego or TA's "I'm OK—you're OK" or Gestalt's awareness or Glasser's responsible behavior or the process-identity model presented here, the danger remains the same. This danger is that therapists will not be satisfied with the role of problem solvers; they may insist on being philosophical gurus. Their major concern seems to be not the help they can offer to those with troubling symptoms but rather the teaching of a new life style. Helping professionals are commonly humanistic priests and ministers.

There is value in having a functional model in contrast to which the professional can evaluate dysfunctional behavior, a model that offers a means of exploring himself for his own growth and sensitivity. But it is quite another matter to imagine that the model should be imposed upon one's clientele. On occasion clients sincerely raise philosophical issues for therapeutic exploration. By and large, however, most clients are interested primarily in getting over their painful symptoms and on with the process of daily living. A client's bid for self-understanding and life-style exploration is usually not a philosophical quest at all but rather a plea for a long-term dependency relationship with the therapist and a readiness to make the therapist into a guru with whom he can identify, and whom he can imitate. This is the client's notion of how he will reduce the pain in his life. Unfortunately, many lonely, unhappy therapists have an equal need to assume such a role. Even when a client seeks symptom relief, he is commonly seduced into a ''philosophical quest'' by the insecure therapist who suggests that his *real* problem lies elsewhere.

In Chapters 7 to 10, we shall note a number of philosophical implications of the process-identity model and see how this undergirds a significant-other-system (interpersonal) way of understanding pathology. The use of therapeutic techniques is understood from the perspective of engaging the client with his daily life process as rapidly as possible. The goals of client modifiability (Chapter 9) clearly differentiate the varied ways in which clients view their problems and the change process itself. We shall see that the therapist's personal philosophical bias must be repeatedly subordinated to the client's interest, need, and ability-to-use. The therapist must be more of a strategist and less of a guru.

Notes

1. Carlos Castaneda, *A Separate Reality: Further Conversations with Don Juan* (New York: Simon & Schuster, 1971), p. 107.

2. Martin J. Heinecken, *A Moment before God* (Philadelphia: Muhlenberg Press, 1956), pp. 295–304.
3. Frederick Perls, Ralph F. Hefferline, and Paul Goodman, *Gestalt Therapy* (New York: Dell, 1951), pp. 26–27.
4. J. Krishnamurti, *The Awakening of Intelligence* (New York: Harper & Row, 1973), pp. 422–26; Robert A. Margrove, *est: Making Life Work* (New York: Dell, 1976), p. 101.

Chapter 6

Perspectives on Personality Theory

Having developed a philosophical position, let us look at how this translates into personality theory. We shall do this in two ways. The first is to conceptualize personality functioning similar to Freud's id-ego-superego theory for purposes of contrast. Secondly we shall examine the use of theory, questioning both its validity and its utility.

Being Activity

In the philosophical perspective we have developed we have already seen three important points of diversion from psychoanalytic thinking. The first has to do with the dynamo which drives human beings. Freud's id was the repository of those primitive, animal drives developed for purposes of survival. The forces from the id arose within the self as a threat to both personal identity and social interaction.

In contrast, what we have labeled Being Activity functions as a wise id. It is the source of growth and direction, knowing what is best for us at any given moment. We do not have an animal id within us, we rather have the wisdom of the universe within us—mineral, plant, animal, and human. Secondly it is erroneous to say all this is contained within us. It is more accurate to say that Being Activity is itself the total action of our surroundings at any given moment. We experience this Being Activity through the creative and integrative activities that constitute the particular form (in age, size, shape, sex, intelligence, appearance, etc.) called ourself. We know this experience in awareness of our needs, our potentials, and our limitations. What we are actually experiencing is Being Activity as it acts in a unique individual human life form with time–space dimensions. It is quite possible, as we saw in our discussion of process identity in Chapter 2, to experience Being Activity in a wider frame than the limitations of the physical body. What is meant by the natural wisdom of Being Activity is the creative-integrative process that is constantly at work responding to the total forces acting upon us at any given moment. This natural creative-integrative process occurs at an unconscious level and has as its combined purpose informing us of our needs for growth and survival and informing us of our potentials for acting effectively upon the world about us.

Viktor Frankl speaks of man as being "summoned by life" in viewing his life as a personal assignment or mission. Medard Boss similarly describes man as being "claimed" by his surrounding world. He says that

> ... this primary awareness of Being-ness is as the most fundamental feature of man's existence, not an attitude or a property which man has, but that man is this primary awareness of Being-ness, that he is in the world essentially and primarily as such. Man, then is a light which illuminates whatever particular being comes into the realm of its rays. It is of his essence to disclose things and living beings in their meaning and content.[1]

Man's sense of conscience is founded upon the necessity of giving himself creatively and sensitively to the world about him. He can authentically exist only in this responsive relation.

Frankl also relates man's primary responsibility—his basis for meaning—to his act of momentary relation. One seeks the perspective of the utter singularity (one-timeness) of any given situation as well as the uniqueness of his always changing person in response to the situation.[2] The situation and the person are inseparable in the achievement of human meaning.

With both Boss and Frankl, we see that man's sense of meaning stems from an inseparable linkage between the integrating and creative forces within himself and the life situation through which he moves. The ego's sense of responsibility is based upon this perspective. Note how this way of thinking differs from a conception of the ego as primarily seeking its own pleasure or lessening anxiety. Frankl makes the specific point that man, in his activation of will-to-meaning, will sometimes accept suffering as an inevitable component of discharging his responsibility to himself and the life process. The philosophical concept of courage, Tillich's courage to be, for example, agrees with this insight.

Frederick Perls labels Being Activity, as humanly experienced, as the self. The self is a continuing process of contacting-actualizing-completing of gestalts. Gestalts are the figures (the focus of interest) arising from a background field of total stimuli present at any given moment. The emerging gestalt results from the "Wisdom of the Organism," as Perls calls it, in knowing what must be dealt with next. He defines the self as the contact-boundary of the organism–environment field.[3]

What we have termed here the Being Activity is described by Joseph Nuttin as the dynamic unity underlying all human needs, which operates as a continuing search for contact and vital exchanges—an active openness. He defines needs as types of interaction—a seeking of specific behavioral relationships in the ego-world. Needs are therefore contacts and exchanges as opposed to drives existing within the isolated person. He describes the same activity of openness-to-the-environment with regard to one's biological, social, and existential needs.[4]

According to Nuttin, biological needs are experienced as a break in the organic equilibrium of homeostasis in the organism–environment field. Such needs are met both by the automatic regulative process of the organic system and by the behavioral regulative process of the conscious organism responding to its surrounding environment. Needs at the psychosocial level are experienced as a need for social contacts, exchange, communication, support, sympathy, and self-giving. He emphasizes that a person unfolds his psychic and social personality through active and passive contact with others. The less he concentrates upon himself and the more open he is to others, the better he can maintain and develop himself. The existential need is experienced as a need to maintain, develop, and illuminate his existence. Man is not self-sufficient at any level of needs, according to Nuttin. He finds himself more or less consciously integrated with and supported by the order of reality, and it is by participating in Being itself (as this totality) that his personal existence is created. Man is a core of life continually being fed by contact with the biological, psychosocial, and existential spheres of reality. He is intrinsically bound up with that which is not himself.[5]

Security Image

The concept of the security image incorporates Freud's superego as well as his entire system of defenses. The security image develops in early childhood much as Freud described the emergence of the superego. It is experienced as a system of defensive beliefs, values, assumptions, stereotypes, attitudes, rules. The point of difference is that the security image develops as a result of conscious choice, whereas Freud viewed the development of the superego as largely unconscious and automatic. The advantage of the security image concept is that it is a phenomenological description of an ongoing, active, changing part of our subjective process. The superego, according to Freud, develops first in an externalized fashion and is later internalized. In healthy functioning the superego activity is finally taken over by the ego in the form of a dynamic ego ideal. The conception of the security image emphasizes a continuous process of image idolatry throughout one's lifetime. If one comes to understand how one's superego was formed by parental injunctions and other influences so that one finally reassesses all of one's values and makes them one's own, this is no protection from an ongoing security-image activity. As one image is dispelled, it is quickly replaced by a new image that is for the same security-preserving, growth-resisting purpose as was the previous image. A common example of this is the authoritarian cockiness evident in people who have completed an analysis or some other intense program of self-development, whether through therapy, religion, or some type of growth group experience. Their self-model of "maturity" becomes the new security image form used to control both themselves and others.

A more accurate description of the security image is to see it as really a series of subimages. Each subimage has its own emotional charge, is triggered by certain kinds of circumstances, and is fortified by a system of related beliefs, attitudes, and values usually experienced in the form of "inner chattering" of thought process or by imaginary images. At one time you are the romantic lover, at another the powerful authority, still another time you are the bumbling parent, then you will be the shy or inept socializer, and so forth. There are images of attraction or desire and there are images we prefer to avoid. The "multiple personality" syndrome that has fascinated novelists on occasion is really an exaggeration of a process that is common to us all. The sense of identity, of having an ego or self, is the boundary our mind seeks to construct in order to encompass our many, oftentimes conflicting, subimages. It is this surrounding boundary that may be dissolved by either the no-mind or panic–apathy–rage states of mind.

Subimages as well as an overriding identity need not be defensive. This image construction activity of the mind can be useful as we engage in situations that require varied roles. The pragmatic self can play with such images, using them and discarding them at will. The security image clings to its subimages with catastrophic expectations as to what might occur if the image is lost or altered.

The purpose of the security image is the preservation of individual identity. It is the survival need in human form. It is based upon the premise that one is essentially isolated, unconnected, rootless, alone, helpless, and must therefore control both subjective and interpersonal interaction so as to secure a place in the world, or even in eternity. It is a carryover of the infant's initial experience of self-awareness while in a helpless state of total dependency. The "life-and-death" importance of security-image control efforts results in the recurring interference with the relational (growth) promptings of Being Activity.

According to Perls, the ego establishes a "mind" (also described as "maya," character, a computer), which resembles the security image described here. The purpose of this "mind" is to furnish a symbol of identity using such means as fantasy, illusion, desensitizing the sensoric system, shrinking the ego boundary, fragmentation of personality into "top dog"-"underdog" components, exaggeration and projection of feelings, repression of certain expressions of needs, and devitalizing the organism generally. All this is to protect the person from experiencing suffering—anxiety and panic related to a sense of nonbeing, having no identity, which Perls describes as experiencing the "hole" behind the false "mind."

However, when the ego permits the self-activity to occur directly, Perls likens this to the "satori" experience of Zen. The person lets himself "explode" in direct contact—through joy, grief, anger, or orgasm. One loses his "mind" and is now simply process, direct happening in the here and now. He allows himself to move with life, being in fundamental balance, harmony, and relation with what occurs.[6]

Perls's concept of an interfering "mind" is quite similar to conceptualizations by Carl Rogers and the encounter group theorists. The notion in common, here, is that this selflike structure is established by accepting certain traits and characteristics of the personality and rejecting, denying, and projecting other parts—generally the opposite components (Everett Shostrom's and Perls's "top dog" and "underdog"). The accepted parts are exaggerated and elevated in importance, for they become the way of experiencing identity. Interestingly enough, the theory of change for most of these writers is not that of analyzing the operation of the "mind" but rather encouraging direct contact with and activation of the "missing parts of self." It is this alive, healthy encounter (allowing natural contacting and actualizing) that provides the motivation for freeing oneself further from the dominating influence of "mind." One need not understand the causal factors determining "mind," for one simply desires to reject its interference out of preference for the more direct, satisfying experience of relation or actualization.

Jung's theory of personality bears strong resemblance to the thinking of gestalt psychology. Basic to his theory is his concept of the opposites, the opposing forces of personality. He equates ego with consciousness and sees the ego's primary task as differentiation (identity of oneself as an individual). The "persona" is the outgrowth of the ego's adaptive efforts aimed at differentiation. The persona can take the realistic form of the ego ideal, as defined herein, or it can take the defensive form of the security image. When it acts in the latter way, Jung terms it the "persona mask." The persona mask develops by identifying with and exaggerating certain aspects of personality while repressing and denying other aspects (similar to the "top dog" and "underdog" theory of Perls and Shostrom). The repressed and denied parts of personality are termed the "shadow." Jung points out three areas where this process occurs. The first is the extrovertive or introvertive attitude toward self-expression. The second area involves the basic ego functions of thinking, feeling, intuition, and sensation. One of these will become the exaggerated mode of living, while its opposite (thinking/feeling, intuition/sensation) will be the function repressed. The other two usually will be permitted some moderate expression. The third area is the animus-anima, the masculine or feminine components of personality. The persona mask results from identifying with one aspect in each of these three different areas while rejecting the opposite.

Jung viewed neurosis not only in the negative light of revealing a "complex" or residual conflict of childhood but also in a positive way. Libido (life force) carries with it a synthesizing function, so that a neurosis is an individual's maladopted way of seeking integration of opposing forces within himself. Jung called the libido force toward creativity and toward the experience of meaning Spirit or Soul. This force operates through the "archetypes," which are experienced in symbolic forms by the person (often identified through his dreams, his art, and the meanings he derives from his religion). An archetype is energy or power aimed at integrating the opposites of personality. Jung found the symbolic process of revealed archetypes to have common patterns among all cultures. This finding substantiated his idea of a universal unconsciousness.

Jung sees the personality as responding constructively to these archetypes in two ways. They may be perceived in symbolic form, such as through myths and religious symbols that take on a highly personal meaning for the individual and by which he senses and accomplishes his own possibility for integration. Religious ritual may serve this purpose, although Jung recognized the decline in effect and value of traditional religious symbols. The other form is what Jung terms individuation, described as a very difficult, painful, often dangerous process, which may be accomplished through psychotherapy or by religious experience.

In the process of individuation, Jung uses the term "Self" to mean an emerging awareness of a new center of personality. In the terminology of personality, as described here, the awareness of Self would be the ego's realization that it is not the sole director of personality but is rather the co-worker with Being. Identity is transferred from the security image to Being awareness.

In Jung's thinking, the Self emerges in order to unify the polarities of personality and bring the person to an acceptance of the wholeness of himself. Conscious and unconscious are synthesized and the "shadow" is incorporated with the conscious Self. This process occurs when the individual expands his awareness of his dreams, reveries, moods, and sometimes the symbolic forces emerging from his involvement with art and religion. This new center, the Self, not only is seen as the center of his own personality but is identified with the center of all forms of existence—with the life process itself. Jung comments on this experience:

> This psychological fact could best be expressed in the words: it is not I who lives, it lives me. The illusion as to the superior powers of the conscious leads me to the belief: I live. If the recognition of the unconscious shatters this illusion, the former appears as something objective in which the ego is included.[7]

Ego

The two critical differences between ego functioning and Freudian theory have already been set forth. The first point is that the ego is a conscious, choosing, meaning-making center, inevitably responsible for its conclusions as it interacts with its environment. This does not mean that subjective activities do not occur outside of ego awareness; but when they do it is a result of the ego's having at some time chosen to keep certain cues outside of conscious awareness.

The second point of difference has to do with the executive function of the ego in relation to personality functioning. As we saw in our discussion of no-mind/pragmatic-self interplay, the ego serves an important function in the world of dichotomized relationships. It is not the executive, however, in that it does not do all the deciding. As we have seen, Being activity presents needs and potentials to the ego in the form of relational or growth promptings. It is the ego's decision how it will respond to such promptings, particularly when they also conflict with security-image strivings. Integration and creativity occur through Being activity, and the ego can then choose how to act in relation to these promptings. But who really is in charge? As Jung indicated, we are more lived by immersion in the interaction of life process than we are directing the living. Ego and Being Activity are working partners, with ego taking more the follower than the leader role.

Andras Angyal speaks of the fundamental tendency of personality toward increased autonomy, expressed as spontaneity, self-assertiveness, striving toward freedom and mastery. This he calls self-determination. The other tendency, labeled self-surrender, is a seeking to become part of something conceived to be greater than or beyond oneself. He unites these two by pointing out that in the effort toward increased autonomy one discovers this cannot be achieved effectively by force but rather must be sought through obedience, understanding, and respect for the laws of the environment.[8]

Joseph Nuttin describes the maturing process as harmonizing the intimate sphere and social structure of personality, so that the intimate part (subjectivity) is no longer a frustrated ego and the social part is no longer a mask of social interaction. In discussing the intimate experience, he says:

> The self must accept positively all the personal characteristics, possibilities, insufficiencies, and impossibilities which it discovers and experiences in the most intimate depth of its own nature. He accepts the task of becoming himself and of constructing for himself a life and a personality from the data which he finds within himself.[9]

Nuttin differentiates this intimate sphere from Freud's unconscious or preconscious. He points out that it is usually inaccessible, as one lives most of the time at the level of social masks (security-image operation). Yet the intimate sphere is not really unconscious: We are simply failing to give our attention to it. He describes appropriate attention as requiring "a certain sincerity and simplicity toward all the data of personality."[10]

Nuttin points out that "the ability to concentrate on some activity (attention), to the complete forgetfulness of Self, is what is meant by the psychic gift of Self to the object."[11] He goes on to emphasize that one gives oneself in one's aim or intention—creating a wide receptivity to the other, whatever form the other might take. To do this effectively requires that one free oneself from egotistical concerns (security-image domination) to some degree. "People and things act upon us from all directions because our organism opens out upon the world in all directions. Any concrete situation affects us in all these ways at once and invites or compels us to reply to it by some kind of reaction—our behavior.[12] This concept is similar to that of Viktor Frankl, who terms the living of life as an assignment—one is questioned by life, and our purpose as men is to respond by actualizing the potential values of our own uniqueness when encountering a specific situation.[13]

Existential Perspectives

It is inaccurate to link a particular group of psychotherapists and theoreticians with the existential perspective. Different groups have emphasized different aspects of existential thinking. At least four groupings seem necessary to encompass the influence of existentialism in modern psychotherapy practice: analytic, awareness-oriented, reality-oriented, and interpersonal.

The analytic group, which includes Medard Boss, Ludwig Binswanger, and Rollo May, has emphasized the importance of understanding the unique "world view" of the client as he experiences it phenomenologically, as opposed to clinical categorizations based upon "objective" descriptions of reality as seen by the therapist.

The awareness-oriented group is a broad classification incorporating most of the "humanistic" or "third force" group of practitioners. The emphasis here is on the natural integrative, creative, growth force at the core of personality. The emphasis of treatment is upon heightened awareness within the interview that will nurture clarity of relational or growth promptings, at the same time helping the client to realize how he habitually blocks or avoids such awareness. This group includes Carl Jung, Karen Horney, Eric Fromm, Andras Angyal, Abraham Maslow, Prescott Lecky, Clark Moustakas, Carl Rogers, Joseph Nuttin, Sidney Jourard, Arthur Burton, Leslie Farber, Alan Wheelis, and Gordon Allport. Rollo May is associated with this group as well as with the analytic group. The recent growth-group movement, incorporating encounter, gestalt, psychodrama, TA, TM, est, psychosynthesis, and transpersonal therapies, is clearly related to this emphasis upon awareness.

The reality-oriented group includes William Glasser, Albert Ellis, Hobart Mowrer, Willard Mainord, Camilla Anderson, Victor Frankl, and such self-help groups as Alcoholics Anonymous and Synanon. The emphasis in this group is upon clarifying and actualizing choices as rapidly as possible so that the person begins to do something about altering his problem rather than remain at either the cognitive or the feeling level. The focus on choice, value clarification, and responsibility links this group of therapists with the existential stance. Values and beliefs are focused upon in order to help the client see how these are actively impairing certain aspects of his growth-need satisfaction.

Finally, there is the interpersonal group—primarily the communication–general-system-theory group associated with the development of family therapy, paradoxical strategies, and brief psychotherapy at the Palo Alto institute. This group includes Gregory Bateson, Don Jackson, Jay Haley, Paul Watzlawick, John Weakland, and Richard Fisch. The communication process linking man with his surrounding world is described much as the existentialists present it. Man creates his own meanings out of such interchanges and is fully responsible for the world he creates. It is out of this self-created world that man makes his choice of behavior, which in turn affects the world about him. "Life—or reality, fate, God, nature, or whatever name one prefers to give it—is a partner whom we accept or reject, and by whom we feel ourselves accepted or rejected, supported or betrayed. To this existential partner, perhaps even as much as to a human partner, man proposes his definition of self and then finds it confirmed or disconfirmed; and from this partner man endeavors to receive clues about the "real" nature of their relationship."[12] This group views psychopathology as an expression of the current interactional system of the person's life. His significant others are inevitably involved in treatment, either directly or indirectly.

As we shall see in the next chapter regarding the significant-other system, knowledge of personality functioning is most useful in understanding one's present life style, mode of adjustment and symptom utilization. Early historical trauma may help clarify our understanding of a person, but need not be the focus of concern in producing change.

Symptoms can be understood as ways of managing either one's relationships with significant others (games and control efforts for some semblance of love or attention) or dealing with one's own security image (self-stroking, self-pity, excuses for inadequate functioning). The latter effort is also related to ineffective validation in our current significant-other system.

Symptoms have been learned and associated with specific defensive subimages. So long as they are productive and reinforced, they will persist. This is not to say that one is totally determined by one's significant-other system. As we have observed in the process of Being Activity one experiences creative and integrative growth strivings that stem from our total realm of awareness. At times the significant others in our lives may need to change or risk being discarded in order to make room for an important unique potential that has emerged in ourself.

The treatment emphasis varies among these four groupings. Analytic is primarily individual; awareness and reality utilize both individual and group modalities; communication–general-systems emphasizes marital and family groupings.

The Use and Abuse of Personality Theory

The existentialists have been critical of the particular uses of personality theory on the basis of its questionable premises of objectivity. The model that is the target of their criticism is the one commonly experienced in mental-health and social-agency consultations, in which case staff spends 90 percent of discussion time in theoretical speculation and about 10 percent on strategies for change. This model emphasizes, first, the collection of appropriate historical data; second, the formulation of a dynamic-diagnostic description of intrapsychic functioning—as complete as possible; and, third, conclusions drawn from this picture regarding treatment prognosis, goals, and appropriate techniques.

From the existential viewpoint, the dangers of this approach are the subjugation of the client to a theory that in itself can never fully explain him. Furthermore, such a model is based upon the therapist's own definition of healthy functioning, which is used to understand and influence the client's perception of himself. Therapy is not so much a problem-solving process as a means of indoctrinating clients with a philosophy or life-style perspective, one that originates with the therapist rather than the client himself. Even in those therapies focused primarily upon the expression of subjective experience—such as psychoanalysis and gestalt—the therapist clarifies when, where, and how a client is stuck in repetitive defensive processes. The very assertion by the therapist that the client is stuck or is being defensive is itself a comment about how the client is living in contrast to some model that defines how he could or should be living. Such ideals as ego autonomy, I'm OK—you're OK, authenticity, responsible awareness, and adequate meeting of needs for love and self-adequacy are all models of health with which the client must compare himself. In this regard, even many of the existential writers mentioned above fall into the same category: therapists as philosophical promoters.

There may be a legitimate place in psychotherapy for philosophical promotion, when clients specifically seek this kind of help. So long as the therapist is clear with the client about his own philosophical position and the client willingly seeks to understand and adopt the therapist's frame of reference, there may be no problem.

More commonly, however, clients seek the help of social workers and other therapists in relation to specific troubling symptoms or problems. The exploration of these symptoms is done by the therapist in such a manner as to imply that the *real* problem is not the presenting one but some underlying difficulty having to do with the client's life style (defense system, choice making, need-meeting, avoidance processes). Even then therapy might be legitimized by the therapist as representing a particular psychological-philosophical perspective that may be of help to the client's growth and resolution of his problems. More commonly, however, the therapist simply asserts his authoritative role (often quite subtly) by the message that he knows how the client is creating his difficulties and can help him understand himself more objectively and effectively. It is the self-understanding component of this message that hooks the client into cooperating with the therapist's philosophical perspective, which itself has never been clarified.

There is an alternative model of treatment which avoids the self-understanding gambit altogether. This model, which might be defined as the problem-solving process, has been developed by the communication–general-systems group mentioned above. Paul Watzlewick, in his book *Change,* constructs this model from group theory and the theory of logical types. The focus is upon the change process itself rather than on understanding in detail the intrapsychic dynamics of the client.*[14] In this regard it also resembles behavior modification.

In contrast to the data-dynamics, prognosis, goals, techniques model described above, the problem-solving model looks at problem factors of interacting systems impeding change and strategies to deal with existing change efforts differently. In this model both interpersonal patterns and intrapsychic patterns (motivations, beliefs and attitudes, avoidances) are considered, but only in relation to the client's currently frustrating efforts to change his problematic situation. A full description of personality functioning is unnecessary and even diverts the focus of therapy. "Second-order change" is the major interest on the part of the therapist.

---

*The problem-solving process of Watzlawick is not to be confused with Helen Harris Perlman's "problem-solving process," familiar to social workers Perlman is rooted in understanding problems from an intrapsychic framework. Watzlawick sees problems as resulting from the very way in which they are defined and struggled with, which produces no change. See Paul Watzlawick, John Weakland, and Richard Fisch, *Change: Principles of Problem Formation and Problem Resolution* (New York: W. W. Norton, 1974).

This involves altering the existing change-effort process, which has been ineffective and actually maintains the symptom or problem. Therapy takes the form of specific tasks, often paradoxical in nature, that enable the client to deal with the change process itself in a new way. The issue of self-understanding is bypassed or else utilized briefly in the "reframing process," which is the therapist's effort to make the proposed tasks palatable to the client. The therapist has no model of health that he seeks to teach the client. He simply seeks to release the client from his self-made-problem imprisonment so that he can go on with his life in whatever way he desires.

The problem-solving model is profoundly existential in that it accepts and indirectly affirms the client's life style and philosophy, no matter what they may be. The therapist's role is clearly that of an expert in problem-solving rather than a disguised guru. This model is perhaps the most useful for social workers who wish to counteract the negative public image of social workers, which views them as essentially paternalistic, seeking to impose their values and life styles upon others.

There would appear to be a limitation to the problem-solving model. To insist that values, heightened awareness, and self-understanding are beyond the legitimate scope of the therapist's work seems as constricting as to insist that self-understanding is what therapy is all about. The existentialists have asserted that a common modern malady is alienation, anomie, the disruption of values, commitment, choice, and responsibility. If schools and churches are not effectively handling this philosophical dilemma in modern man, perhaps the helping professions generally should share in the effort. While it may be affirming to accept the client's existing philosophy and life style, the fact remains that many clients will express personal dissatisfaction in these areas. So long as the therapist recognizes his own limitations in the philosophical-religious arena and is straightforward about the perspective he might offer as one helpful effort, then the pursuit of self-understanding and growth will appear to be a legitimate activity among helping professionals.

The issue coming to the fore here is that of therapeutic dogmatism versus client-centered responsiveness. As we indicated in the opening chapter, helping professionals have a need to be guiding authorities for others. This very tendency often blinds them to the particular needs of the client seeking help. In the next four chapters I shall examine the complexity of the therapist's challenge. How can he be of helping service without impairing the client's growth, encouraging conformity as well as alienation and finding satisfaction in what he does, no matter what the client's response to his therapeutic efforts?

Notes

1. Medard Boss, *Psychoanalysis and Daseinanalysis* (New York: Basic Books, 1963), p. 37.

2. Viktor Frankl, *The Doctor and the Soul* (New York: Alfred A. Knopf, 1955), p. 72.

3. Frederick Perls, Ralf Hefferline, and Paul Goodman, *Gestalt Therapy* (New York: Delta Books, 1951), p. 229.

4. Joseph Nuttin, *Psychoanalysis and Personality* (New York: Mentor Omerga, 1962), pp. 224–35.

5. *Ibid.,* pp. 229–57.

6. Frederick Perls, *Gestalt Therapy Verbatim* (Lafayette, California: Real People Press, 1969), pp. 5–79.

7. C. G. Jung, *Psyche and Symbol* (New York: Doubleday Anchor Books, 1958), p. 347.

8. Andras Angyal, ''A Theoretical Model for Personality Studies,'' in Clark Moustakas, ed., *The Self* (New York: Harper & Row, 1956), p. 49.

9. Nuttin, *Psychoanalysis and Personality,* p. 209.

10. *Ibid.,* p. 219.

11. *Ibid.,* p. 242.

12. *Ibid.,* p. 159.

13. Frankl, p. 66.

14. Paul Watzlawick, Janet Helmick, and Don Jackson, *Pragmatics of Human Communication* (New York: W. W. Norton, 1967), pp. 259–60.

Chapter 7

The Significant-Other-System Perspective

A clear implication of the process-identity perspective is that man's most fundamental need is for meaningful relation with forms of life other than himself. This relation is experienced as connection or rootedness. Zen's realization reveals that life is perfect, complete just as it is, and that man is one with this process.

In terms of psychological theory, we see that the need for relation takes us to a point of understanding man that is beyond Freud's need for pleasure, Adler's need for power, Maslow's need for self-actualization, or Frankl's need for meaning.[1] We are closer to the interpersonal theorists and systems thinking of Sullivan, Fromm, Horney, Bateson, and Jackson.

The psychology of process-identity as we have explored it suggests two ways of experiencing life. Figure 7-1A represents the no-mind/pragmatic-self interplay in which we see ourselves as an interacting process in a world of differentiated forms. While aware of our individuality, we see it as rooted in a wider process of interacting forms. The yin-yang symbol in the center represents the wisdom of the organism—our needs, potentials, unfinished business. The second circle represents the ego, or pragmatic self. The third circle represents the security image—the protective activities of personality that build belief systems, val-

Figure 7.1

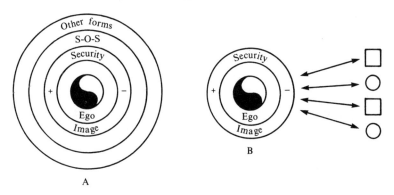

ues, assumptions, stereotypes, and judgments around both positive and negative notions about one's own identity. Here is the
source of fear and desire (minus and plus signs). The next circle
(S-O-S) is one's significant-other system, which usually includes
family, relatives, and friends. The outermost circle represents the
vast variety of other forms of life affecting the person; other
people (strangers, enemies, acquaintances, fellow workers,
neighbors, members of groups), the world of nature, the world of
material objects, the world of ideas from others (literature, news
media, philosophy, history).

Figure 7-1B represents the ego-identity model, in which the
individual is essentially isolated in a world of isolated forms.
While there is interaction between these forms (represented by
the double arrows), each is essentially alone, alienated from the
others.

It is the first model of personality as a single, inclusive, interacting system that we shall examine here. This model can also
be illustrated as in Figure 7-2, which more clearly delineates the
components of process activity. The outer circle represents one's
world of awareness; it is a personally constructed world made up
of meanings concluded as a result of interaction with other forms
of life during one's personal history of being alive. One is fully
responsible for this world in the sense that he has created it

through the meanings he has bestowed. While he may not have created all the forms or forces with which he has interacted, he remains responsible for the meanings concluded about these interactions.

In Figure 7-2 A represents the activity of both attitudes and awareness on the part of the person. Attitudes come from beliefs or meanings concluded. Awareness is one's total comprehension of any given moment, offering him choice points as to what he will do next in relation to his world. Arrow B represents behavior; here are our choices as to how we will affect the world at any given moment. Arrow C represents the communication, the interactional feedback, from the world in response to our behavior. Here is the possibility of dialogue, which in turn can affect our attitudes about ourselves and thus shift our way of experiencing. This A-B-C activity is the process flow of life as experienced by the individual.

One's experience of meaningful relation stems from the ongoing activity of these three components, when such interaction produces a sense of vitality, caring, need satisfaction, creative expression. This was apparent in our discussion of process identity in Chapter 2. When, on the other hand, interaction of these components is stifled through maneuvers of interpersonal games, then the individual experiences alienation, boredom, and isolation. The interpersonal flow of life process can be disrupted by either subjective (attitude-awareness) or interpersonal (behavior-communication feedback) rigidity and control.

Figure 7.2

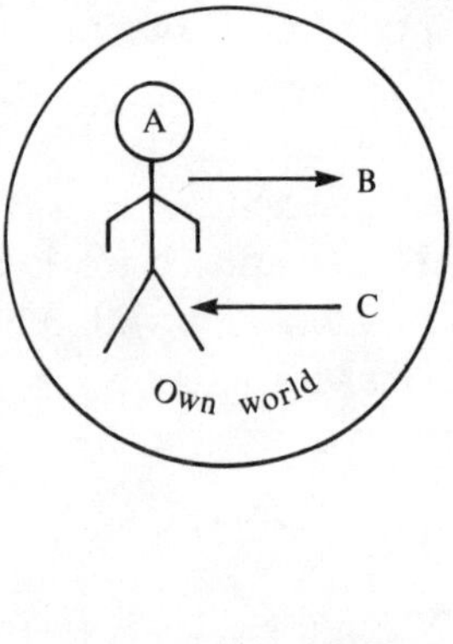

A: Meaning concluded
B: Choices and actions
C: Communication feedback

In discussing the life of dialogue, Martin Buber points out that the I-Thou relation may occur with one's world of nature, or of ideas, or of other people. He emphasizes, however, that the most important form of relation is with other people.[2]

While it is true that the saint or mystic may be in a state of vitalized relation while living alone in his mountain hut, it is doubtful that he could have arrived at such a point of realization without first having satisfactorily experienced meaningful human dialogue of mutual affirmation.

What we see in such religious figures as Jesus, Moses, and Buddha is that, even though a portion of their lives involved a personal search of inwardness and isolation from others, all three affirm a life style that finally requires highly personal, caring interactions with others. Buddha renounces nirvana out of compassion for others; Christ submits to the cross out of love for others; Moses continues to struggle with his rebellious community in order to lead them out of the desert.

The concept of the significant-other system is therefore crucial for understanding the individual's efforts to find and be himself. It is within interactional exchanges with significant others that the individual allows the fullest expression of himself, as a responsive, affecting part of this interpersonal system. Christ proclaimed the greatest commandments to be: "Thou shalt love the Lord thy God with all thy heart and with all thy soul and with all thy mind" and "Thou shalt love thy neighbor as thyself." While it may be possible for a few people to expand their significant-other system to include more and more people, and eventually the whole of mankind, this is certainly the rare exception. What we see with most people who declare their love and devotion for all of humanity is an avoidance of dealing with the significant others in their lives in a genuinely dialogical way. Such "humanitarians" are usually in love with an idea that affirms their own security image and provides them an escape from the personal world of sincerity and struggle of dialogue.

Figure 7-3 is another representation of the process flow of the individual and his world, clearly emphasizing the significant-

Figure 7.3

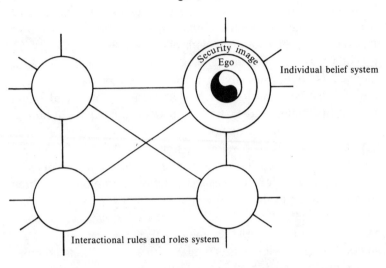

other system of which he is a part. In this diagram we see three significant others in the individual's life. While both the individual and others have many additional connections in their worlds of work, play, socializing, organization, and so forth, it is most important to understand this significant-other system if one is to understand the individual. The social worker, of all helping professionals, should be most appreciative of this way of appraising individual functioning. He must see the constant interdependence of the person's subjective system of beliefs, attitudes, values, assumptions, and priorities, and the significant-other system of rules and roles that defines how this group of people will interact—their expectations of one another, their agreements out of which come trust, commitments, games, and manipulations.

Significant others are defined as those people who have been invested with identity-survival significance by the individual. The security image was originally developed by his engagement with the significant-other system (from now on designated S-O-S) of his early childhood. Even when this image had been altered, this inevitably involved engagement with significant others. Sometimes the original parental or familial system produced such image alteration by the very fact that the significant others had themselves undergone change. At other times, image change occurred as a result of the input of new significant others in the individual's life. Self-identity and one's currently active S-O-S are inevitably intertwined.

As one moves beyond one's family of origin to peer relationships and eventually to the establishment of one's own family or system of nonfamilial significant others, one seeks out people who will shore up one's sense of identity in a way one believes it must be affirmed. Those whom one chooses are seeking the same social affirmation in relation to their own identities. Thus a system of complementarity is established.

The S-O-S becomes the basis for ongoing growth among its members when dialogical exchanges are permitted. It also becomes the basis for impeding growth when rigid security-control efforts predominate. "Dialogue" refers to a mutuality and genuineness of interchange. People give each other room to be themselves, yet at the same time they listen and learn from one another. One needs the caring interest and acceptance of others to test out his own emerging attitudes and feelings. When the S-O-S is threatened by new ideas or emotional expression, it asserts controls that may impair individual growth.

Change can occur in two ways, or by a combination of both. The individual may alter his own attitudes as well as awareness so as to assert his behavior in some new way to the significant others in his life. In this case the significant others must themselves begin to change in response to the new assertion of the individual. If such change fails to occur, the individual initiating change will either retreat to his former position or leave the S-O-S for some other S-O-S that will accept him.

The second way of change is for the others to alter their way of responding to an individual within their system. This results in a change in the individual's attitudes and feelings; his identity system is shaken. He is more likely to alter his own subjective belief system (security-image identity) than to leave the system if change was initiated by others rather than by himself. If he refuses to change, the significant others may return to their previous modes of interaction or else eject him from the system.

Family-therapy theorists have correctly postulated that the most powerful of these change forces is usually the system itself rather than the individual within the system. Pathological symptoms are understood as conflicts between the individual's growth needs and his defensive system, which inevitably involves his efforts to preserve his identity and to maneuver his significant others so as to maintain a sense of affirmed identity. Symptoms along with attitudes and feelings will be altered as a result of a shift in the rules and roles defining system interactions. When several members of an S-O-S are involved in changing their interpersonal behavior, the entire system is opened up for new appraisals of needs, potentials, and limitations on the part of its members.

The data necessary for understanding an individual's problems must include the following areas:

1. The nature of the S-O-S operation of rules (communication patterns) and the roles that sustain it. Who is in the system? How does it operate? What do people do to one another in the process of meeting needs (expectations, stereotyping, game maneuvers)?

2. The wider systems effecting the S-O-S: economics, work, school, church, relatives and friends, forces of social oppression, etc. Here we might want to consider the potential or opportunities for building a new S-O-S for the individual, if need be.

3. The belief system of the individual or individuals seeking help—attitudes, values, assumptions, judgments, the way in which he or they seek to identify himself or themselves as worthwhile.

4. The avoidance system that impedes awareness: suppression, projection, etc., used to handle one's fear in relation to the loss of some prized identity.

5. The interplay between attitudes, awareness, avoidance, and the way in which the S-O-S operates (roles, games).

While history may be of some importance at arriving at an understanding of these factors, the principal concern is the present interaction system.

The major thrust of the S-O-S perspective is that the individual's primary need is for meaningful relation, for engaging connection with important other people in his life now. To deal with intrapsychic change itself as aiming at new knowledge, pleasure, power, or meaning is insufficient. A new form of relational engagement must result. Life process is vitalized through relation, not cognition.

The active S-O-S in an individual's life may take one of several forms. For some people, there is no current S-O-S of which they are an interactive part. The elderly, for example, commonly live out their significant-other interaction through memory. They may even talk to these remembered figures reliving past memories. For others, the significant others are an active part of their life, but are at a distance geographically, and the interchange is primarily by letter, telephone, and occasional visits. There are three forms of existing significant others. The first is the active group of family, relatives, or friends. The second is the psychotic's "imagined" relational contacts with forces or "others" that inhabit his psychic world. The third takes the form of generalized and distorted significant others, as in cases where the individual substitutes some social institution for more personal relationships. Thus the military service, the hospital staff, a self-help group, a jail, or an institution for the retarded or the insane may become familylike substitutes. Finally there are some enlightened individuals who relate to the world of nature, of ideas, of humanity in general as genuine significant others. There can also be, of course, combinations of these S-O-S forms.

One needs to understand how the S-O-S operates for an individual in order to know best how to work with him. As we have seen, with the psychotic and psychopath, the therapist must be able to appreciate and validate the world view of the client before there can be any hope of helping him to move in some altered direction.

Emotional Dysfunction as Alienation

Nearly all emotional problems can be understood as forms of alienation—of a breakdown, disruption, or dysfunctioning of the current significant-other system in a person's life. This includes the usual diagnostic categories of psychoses, character disorders, neuroses, and adjustment reactions. The possible exceptions to this would be where the causal factors arc physiological or severe environmental stress threatening physical and safety needs. Yet even in these exceptions, the significant-other relationship system can be the most important factor in helping a person cope with his distressing circumstances.

There are four major sources of alienation (emotional dysfunctioning):

1. *Failure of confirmation by significant others.* Here one's present significant-other system is ineffective in its caring, loving, affirming functions of valuing the uniqueness of the client. Games and maneuvers are used to control the person as a stereotyped object in order to gratify someone else's need. The client himself usually participates in the same activity, using others in such a way that he fails to confirm them as valued human beings in their own right. Family therapists, group therapists, and marriage counselors have provided us with considerable data to exemplify this form of alienation.

2. *Deception over value conflicts.* Values can be understood in an interpersonal context: a person's values provide a set of expectations about him for the significant others in his life. It is this system of consistent behavioral expectations under given sets of circumstances that is basic for people's capacity to trust one another. O. Hobart Mowrer has postulated that guilt over violation of shared values is the cause of most emotional problems.[3]

Value conflict occurs in two ways, both of which involve deception and hiding (which Mowrer sees as the cause of distancing and alienation). First is the instance in which a person behaviorally violates values he shares with some significant other but does not reveal his violation (e.g., the spouse who secretly has an affair, even though both espouse sexual fidelity in marriage). Second is the situation of a person who has changed his value position and lives by a new value but without letting the significant other know (e.g., the spouse who secretly has an affair because he now believes such behavior to be legitimate, although his spouse still believes that they share in common the value of marital fidelity).

3. *Disillusionment, confusion, or loss of personal values.* A person's identity may be shaken, his sense of direction blurred, his choices thwarted by ambivalence and uncertainty when the values he holds dear are revealed to be futile and empty. Insofar as he does not know himself, the significant others in his life no longer know him. Trust is shaken by the uncertainty of expectations. Thus a wife is deeply distressed when her husband undergoes such disillusionment about himself. Will he remain on the job? Will he switch professions? Will he still want me as a wife? Personal identity confusion may easily result in one's distancing oneself from significant others. They are often looked upon with suspicion—as trying to pressure one into conforming again with those values he has now discarded. It is important to understand here that the disillusionment process itself is not the cause of emotional dysfunctioning. Disillusionment involves learning: assessing, discarding, exploring new ideas, experimenting, and assimilating. While painful, it is a natural part of the growth process. It results in emotional dysfunctioning (any number of pathological symptoms) when it interferes with the significant-other system. Value confusion leads to withdrawal or threatening conflicts of social engagement.

4. *Loss of significant others.* Alienation may result from the loss of significant others when there has not yet been sufficient time or opportunity or energy to establish a new significant-other

system in one's life. Loss may occur through death or illness or through relocation, such as a young adult's going away to college or entering military service. Depending upon one's social skills and degree of comfort in seeking new relationships, such losses may result in a period of withdrawal and isolation despite the availability of other people. People's response to such loss experiences may be growth producing or may result in deterioration—depending upon their behavior. Crisis theory provides many examples. Emotional catharsis is often emphasized as an important ingredient of positively managed crises. What is sometimes forgotten is that such catharsis is important insofar as it occurs in the presence of others, so that the feeling expression becomes the means of restoring meaningful contact with other human beings.

The foregoing list leaves out innumerable causal factors usually connected with psychodynamic formulations. If such formulations help us to understand or elaborate upon a person's present mode of existence, particularly his world of significant-other interactions, then by all means we should use them. The four factors described above emphasize a particular perspective in regard to pathology—namely, that if a person is suffering from emotional dysfunction, his problem is active in his present system of relationships; his symptoms do not reflect some historical trauma that has persisted despite a satisfying mode of existence in the present. The attitude of "trauma" theory is most commonly seen among those who treat children individually in play therapy with little or no involvement of the parents because they view the family situation as currently "normal." But if the factors that caused some original trauma have changed and the family is, indeed, "normal" now, then there will be no symptoms. Here we see pathology as actively interpersonal.

But what of a person who lacks any current system of significant others? The problem is not that the person is permanently without significant others in his life. His problem stems from the absence of these relationships and from his avoidance, withdrawal, reluctance, and perhaps limited opportunities in relation to establishing such valued contacts. The concern for change must still relate to the establishment of such a system in his life.

Therapeutic Change Implications

The significant-other-system perspective is, of course, as speculative at this time as any of the other explanations of psychopathology. Yet several useful implications for treatment stem from this perspective and cast doubt on the priority and applicability of various modes of therapy. These implications are important enough to warrant expanded research into the whole matter of what actually produces therapeutic change. The S-O-S perspective suggests that if therapy is to lead to lasting and significant changes, the therapist must understand the significant-other system and seek to mend, restore, replace, or enhance its functioning in the client's life. Let us consider how each of several therapeutic modes can relate to this effort.

1. *Network (tribal) and communal therapies* involve a client's significant-other system in the treatment process in a broader, more intense fashion than any other therapeutic approach. In both network family therapy (Speck) and in the communal form of therapy, exemplified by Synanon, the broad system of significant others in a person's daily life is also a part of the treatment program.[4] The significant others involved in network and communal therapies are part of ongoing relationships, not merely temporary relationships, such as might be involved in hospital "milieu treatment" or in group-therapy programs. In network family therapy, for example, a team of therapists works with a network of people who are intimately involved with a client or family: his family, extended family, relatives, neighbors, friends, and any other helping professionals already involved with the client. How effective and practical these approaches are for most people and agencies is another question, but they are creative efforts to deal as directly as possible with the significant-other system.

Similar to these approaches, although not so extensive in significant-other involvement, are self-help groups: Alcoholics Anonymous, Seven Steppers, Recovery Inc., integrity therapy groups, and cultural identity–commitment groups such as the Black Muslims. Such groups often provide an adjunct system of significant others beyond the family-friends-relatives system. It too is ongoing, in contrast to the temporary nature of therapy or growth groups. Many church organizations are attempting to develop significant-other support systems of this kind.

2. *Family and marital therapies* are therapy forms more easily adapted to agency settings than those mentioned above. In family and marital therapies the most intense, problematic significant others in the person's life are involved in the treatment process. This allows the therapist to understand clearly how the interaction system operates through direct observation and involvement rather than by speculating about it on the basis of the biased hearsay of the individual client. Whether family members are seen as a group for treatment or are treated in varied combinations of individual, couple, group, or family therapy is not so much the issue. What is critical is that the therapist has therapeutic contact with the most significant others in the client's life as part of the ongoing treatment. In most cases, regardless of the presenting problem, family or marital therapy would be the treatment of choice.

3. *Group therapy.* There are occasions when the significant-other system in a client's life cannot or should not be involved in therapy—at least initially. It *cannot* be involved when there are no active significant others in the person's life, or when they are unwilling or unable to participate. There are also situations in which the therapist rightly concludes that the significant-other system is so rigid or destructive that the person would be better seen alone. Significant others *should not* be included when the client himself refuses to enter treatment if these people are involved, or when the client's alienation difficulty has to do with his personal disillusionment—emptiness or deterioration of his own personal values. To involve significant others when the per-

son has not yet found himself—what he wants, needs, values—may force him into premature readjustment to the values of others, which is usually a short-lived solution to his problem. On the other hand, there are times when what appears to be personal value disillusionment is merely a guise and a maneuver to manipulate significant others. This is an example of why the significant-other system must be carefully understood in every instance of treatment.

In the group-therapy situation, the therapist and group become a *temporary* significant-other system for the client. The client may explore and reevaluate himself and his interactions apart from his everyday significant-other system. It is critically important here, however, that the therapy group be seen as a *temporary bridge*, helping the person to reconnect with the significant others in his daily life. It is not enough for the client to understand himself and his group interactions in new ways; the group must take responsibility for helping him understand his everyday significant-other system and begin making efforts to effect change in this system, reporting his results back to the group for reevaluation. It is hoped that at some point the client can move out of group therapy and into family or marital therapy, or else the significant others might be included in the group therapy itself. In some cases the client may gain enough help from the group in understanding and dealing with the significant others in his life to make it unnecessary to involve them directly in the treatment program.

4. *Individual therapy*. The reasons cited for choosing group therapy apply to individual therapy as well: the client cannot or should not involve his significant others in treatment initially. Group therapy has the advantage of helping a client relate to people like his significant-other system; in individual therapy, by contrast, the therapist is the only temporary significant other (and is usually credited by the client with wisdom, maturity, social skills, and self-awareness far beyond the everyday relationships in the client's own life). Individual therapy becomes the treatment of choice when the client refuses treatment that involves

other group members, or where there is no group of clients available. Individual therapy, like group therapy, offers insight, heightened awareness, and opportunities for game-free dialogue or intimacy. The individual therapist is amiss, however, if he fails to seek as accurate an understanding as possible of the client's significant-other system, for the aim of therapy is eventually to help the client effect change in this system. Again, the therapist is but a temporary bridge to the client's everyday S-O-S of relationships. Whenever possible, these significant others should be included in the therapy situation as they or the client are ready for this experience. It is worth postulating that those individual-therapy approaches that do not encourage long-term dependency upon the therapist may be more effective in moving the client toward action with his daily system of significant others.

There are three therapeutic approaches that appear highly questionable from the S-O-S perspective. These are the roles of the therapist as troubleshooter, technician, and facilitator. In all three instances, positive change may occur, but it is highly doubtful that such change will be lasting. When it is lasting, this probably has more to do with happenstance or with a particular client's determination and should not be considered as a success for the therapist.

The therapist-as-troubleshooter is commonly found among harried workers in agencies with unrealistically heavy caseloads. The therapist responds to some cry for help by doing the client's bidding. He is being used on the client's own terms, just as other relatives, friends, family members, and helping people have previously been used, to no avail. The client should not be expected to have a full understanding of the nature of his dilemma and what needs to be done to change it. If he had, he would not need a therapist and already would have secured the help he requires from his available S-O-S.

The therapist-as-technician narrows his focus to a particular problematic symptom without regard for its relation to the client's S-O-S. All symptoms can be viewed as maneuvers to control significant others in one's current life situation. To help a client alter his symptoms without appreciating their function in his S-O-S is merely to effect a shift in symptomatology. The behavior-modifying therapist who claims to have achieved symptom removal without a replacement symptom may be restricting his view of the evidence, just as he restricts his therapy focus. The symptom switch may show up not in the individual client but in the S-O-S. A child may give up bed wetting, for example, but another child in the family may now begin to do poorly in school, or the parents may begin to experience marital strife. The responsible behavior-modifier will maintain an S-O-S perspective in his manner of evaluation and work.

Finally, the therapist-as-facilitator fails to understand his role as a temporary bridge. This therapist says, or implies, that he is there to provide the client with insights, heightened awareness, a corrective emotional experience, or genuine dialogical intimacy, but it is up to the client how he uses this knowledge and experience in his daily life. It is true that the client must choose what he will do with his new learning; however, the therapist bears responsibility for helping the client effect change in his everyday significant-other relationships. Clients will often change through this form of therapy, but certain questions must be raised. The therapist as facilitator offers the client a temporary significant-other relationship in his life. With this adjunct relationship the client may well begin to feel differently about himself and even change his behavior in his daily life. But what happens after termination? Why do so many clients keep coming back to treatment? Why do many clients seek to prolong treatment beyond their apparent need for it? Why do clients frequently move toward divorce following therapy, or else ship their spouses off to therapists following their own termination? It is one thing to alter one's defenses, games, or belief system during the course of a caring relationship with a therapist. It is quite another matter to maintain such changes when, after termination, one's S-O-S no longer includes a therapist. The significant others in one's life are often threatened by the changes that occur with a person. So long as he is in therapy they may tolerate the change simply because he is in "patient" status. The inclusion of at least key significant others in the therapy program is the best preparation for a changed system (and not simply changed ideas).

It is difficult to understand how *social* workers, of all people, became wedded to the individual model. The term "caseworker" should be replaced, because it implies the individual model. Certainly individual long-term treatment is more comfortable for the worker: he is more in control, he can limit his scope of understanding, and caseloads are often more stable and more lucrative in private practice. It may be that social workers who have been analyzed seek to preserve the tie to their own analyst-as-significant-other by dogmatically adhering to what they think is the philosophical and treatment theory of the analyst! They never really resolve termination.

There are subtle ways in which a social worker maintains his individual model, even when believing he is open to S-O-S awareness. A client talks about significant others in his life whom he sees as causing some of his stress. This is an ideal opportunity to discuss involvement of these others in treatment. The gambit used to maintain the individual focus goes something like this: "Since your spouse is not here I cannot change him (or her). Where the wheel squeaks is the place to apply the oil. Let's look at you."

Another maneuver is philosophically rooted. It is the belief that individual intrapsychic exploration is the "deepest" and therefore most significant form of therapy. Analysis is viewed as the epitome of self-understanding and therefore the most profound route to change. The S-O-S perspective not only challenges this belief but even suggests that the individual model fails in understanding and working out the real *present* problem.

A related argument is whether behavior change follows from attitude change or vice versa. Family therapists themselves are divided on this issue: the psychoanalytic against the systems therapists. Since there appears to be evidence that change can occur either way, this would appear to be a needless argument. It would be even worthwhile to explore whether more rapid and longer lasting change might occur by the therapist's combining of the two viewpoints: dynamic understanding and therapeutic efforts including a careful understanding of the rules and roles governing the S-O-S interaction and also of the individual assumptions, beliefs, judgments, and stereotyping of each member of the system. Such factors as culture, motivation, intelligence, and language usage may be important variables in knowing with which clients attitude change should be emphasized and with which one might give priority to behavioral change.

The individual-oriented social worker may be concerned that an S-O-S focus may encourage readjustment or conformity, neglecting the unique growth direction of the individual client. This concern has some validity, as already discussed with regard to clients whose alienation stems from personal disillusionment. However, the reestablishment of direction in one's life is only half the task. The client must still be helped to make new or different connections with an S-O-S beyond the therapist himself. This may sometimes involve a decision to leave one's S-O-S and replace it with another. On the other hand, there may be times when readjustment to one's S-O-S could realistically occur. One may discover that his own perceptions, expectations, and judgments about the significant others in his life are erroneous. In such a case there may be a need not to change others but to change one's own view of interactions that he had been experiencing as painful. But here again, the therapist's knowledge of the actual functioning of the S-O-S is greatly enhanced by direct observation.

The S-O-S perspectives as an expression of an existential way of thinking is an apparent paradox. Perhaps the most individualistic philosophy of all leads to a strong social emphasis. The point to be understood here is that man does not find his happiness or serenity, finally, through his significant others. This he must come upon on his own. Each person makes his peace with his God, with "his world." Yet the significant others in his life are an absolute necessity for him to deal with in his search for truth.

They have survival significance for him to begin with and are required for his personal growth throughout his life. When emotional turmoil arises it is inevitably this system that must be understood.

A shortcoming of all the major writers on existential psychotherapy (including May, Frankl, Binswanger, and Perls) has been their emphasis upon man's search for personal meaning without directly addressing the question of how he comes to express this search with his significant others, and the resulting interpersonal struggles that inevitably arise. Without an emphasis upon engagement with one's S-O-S, therapy that emphasizes a search for meaning tends to encourage the same form of intellectualizing, philosophizing, and self-preoccupation that more traditional insight therapies have focused on. It is one thing to clarify a value stance and live it out in the presence of one's therapist. It is quite another matter to uphold this stance in one's everyday world of significant others after terminating therapy.

Notes

1. Viktor E. Frankl, *The Doctor and the Soul* (New York: Alfred A. Knopf, 1957), pp. 3–26.

2. Martin Buber, *I and Thou* (New York: Charles Scribner's Sons, 1958), pp. 101–103.

3. Hobart Mowrer, *The Crisis in Psychiatry and Religion* (New York: D. Van Nostrand Co., 1961), pp. 81–102.

4. R. Speck and C. Attneave, "Network Therapy," in Andrew Ferber, Marilyn Mendelsohn, and Augustus Napier, eds., *The Book of Family Therapy* (New York: Science House, 1972); Louis Yablonsky, *Synanan: The Tunnel Back* (New York: Penguin, 1967).

Chapter 8

The Enhancement of Change

In addition to the S-O-S perspective on pathology and the use of treatment modes, there are three important principles of treatment stemming from the existential stance. These are experiential change emphasis, client-centered orientation, and personal engagement of the therapist that demonstrates and deal with values, personal feelings, and attitudes. In this chapter we shall explore the emphasis upon experiential change.

In the previous chapter we saw how the interpersonal flow of life process can be disrupted by either subjective (attitudes-awareness) or interpersonal (behavior-communications feedback) rigidity and control. The task of therapy is first to understand how the presenting symptom or problem represents a stoppage in the natural flow of life for the individual or family. Secondly, the therapist seeks to release this flow as rapidly as possible so that the client can return to his everyday tasks of living and growing by using the natural forces in his life system rather than depending on an artificial, temporary significant other like the therapist. Prolonged dependence on the therapist not only delays change and engagement efforts in one's daily life but, as treatment evaluation tends to demonstrate, results in a more pessimistic prognosis.

The client can engage his own life process in a new way subjectively and/or interpersonally—dealing with his attitudes, beliefs, and values as well as his awareness (opening up feelings, sensations, intuition, fantasies, dreams) or altering the rules, roles, and control maneuvers within his S-O-S. While both methods are valuable, when subjective engagement is pursued without an equal emphasis on S-O-S engagement, treatment is only a halfway measure, and the risks of relapse after termination are greater.

Both engagement methods must be designed to enable the client to move as rapidly as possible beyond his control efforts of rigidified dysfunctional attitudes and beliefs, avoidance and suppressive efforts, and his interpersonal stifling methods. Such control efforts are usually maintained by mental activities of self-pity, self-preoccupation, and interpersonal activities of blame and tyrannization of others.

The Role of the Therapist

The role of the therapist has been described in varied ways, depending on the psychotherapeutic model employed. He may present himself as a purveyor of insights (psychoanalytic), a teacher (most reality-oriented therapies), a model (the awareness-oriented, humanistic therapies), a giving parent (supportive approaches), and a rational planner (the task-oriented behavior therapies).

The role of the therapist proposed here is that of a strategist. This means that he may temporarily take on any of the previously mentioned roles, but when he does so he is not representing any particular model of psychotherapy, but rather choosing the route that will most likely produce rapid engagement by the client with his problematic process.

As in most other therapeutic approaches, the worker seeks to form a trusting, caring, positive relationship with the client. It is important for the strategist to accomplish this as rapidly as possible so as to be able to establish a position of power, of influence with the client or family.

The skill of the therapist lies in his ability to form such a positive relationship while at the same time remaining detached from the client's usual efforts to maneuver the therapist. When the therapist is successfully hooked or controlled by the client, then the client uses the therapist just as he uses significant others in his life to stifle any change efforts. This touches on the concept of transference, but that concept is too narrow to explain what most clients do. It is not necessarily control maneuvers that were used with their early parental figures that are brought into the therapeutic game. These maneuvers may have been dropped or altered during the course of the client's life, depending upon the impact of significant others. The client will use whatever control efforts he has found effective with significant others. The client, too, is using power strategies, and when one fails he may bring in a new one.

The therapist's most effective stance for detachment is to accept and affirm the client as he is at the very onset of treatment. He is willing to work with the client toward change but has no investment whatever in whether the client changes or not. He simply makes available his knowledge and skills for the client to use as he pleases. The only exception to this would be in the mutuality of goal setting (Chapter 8) and in occasionally arising value issues, such as suicide, homicide, or child beating, in which certain limits may be set by the therapist (Chapter 10). The therapist's role might be more accurately described as that of a spontaneous strategist. Strategy implies that the therapist is coming from some rationally thought-out, preplanned position. This is partially true in that the therapist continually evaluates the results of interviews and the options open for new efforts. Spontaneity implies the therapist's openness to his own feelings and intuition and his making on-the-spot moves to give expression to them somehow. In this regard the therapist has one important need of his own that requires satisfaction: a need for vitalization, a sense of something actively happening, of helping the client ready himself for some sort of engagement in his problematic style.

Boredom arises in the interviews when the client engages in

endless self-pity, self-justification, blaming of others, or intellectual preoccupation with no goal-directed efforts. Therapists
commonly bore themselves by rationalizing that clients must go
through such deadening maneuvers in order to regroup their defenses. When therapists permit such boredom they are presenting
the client with the same sort of alienated responses he gets from
most others in his life.

Vitalization and the Change Cycle

The choice of therapeutic technique is an outcome of the
therapist's need for vitalization. Strategies come into play as a
means of deciding when and how to employ those techniques that
appear most promising.

The change cycle is illustrated in Figure 8-1. Using the same
concepts described in an individual's life-process flow (Chapter
7), we can see how therapeutic techniques represent varied ways
of producing change. A change of attitude and/or awareness can
produce behavioral change, which in turn can produce new communication feedback. This is the starting place for most of the

Figure 8.1

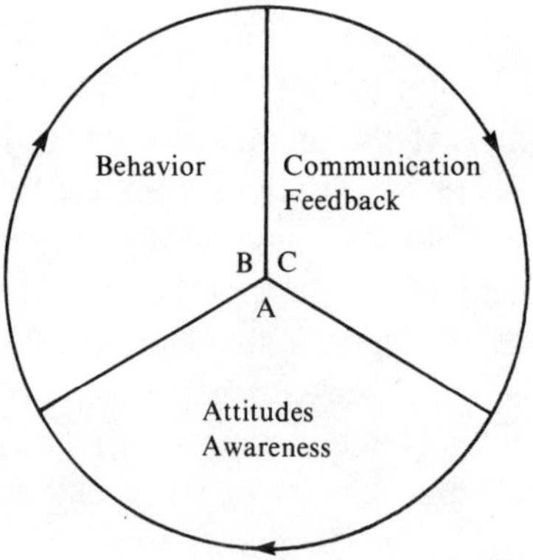

Change cycle

individual psychotherapies, whether they emphasize attitude change (reality, rational emotive, integrity, cognitive, and logo therapies) or awareness change (gestalt, psychodrama, encounter groups, client-centered, psychosynthesis, bioenergetics, and primal scream therapies) or both attitude and awareness change (psychoanalytic, ego psychology, transactual analysis).

However, one might just as well start with behavioral change, which can produce communication-feedback shifts, which in turn can produce changes of attitude and/or awareness. Here is the starting place of behavioral modification and task-oriented approaches such as those described by J. Haley, Milton Erickson, and Paul Watzlawick.

Finally, one may engage the change cycle at the point of communication feedback, as is common in family therapy and marriage counseling, which may result in change of attitude and/or awareness and subsequent behavioral change. Family therapy and marital counseling commonly begin at the interactional level.

Most psychotherapies address all three areas of the cycle, although they tend to emphasize change effort at some particular starting point. The reality-oriented therapies, for example, focus upon attitude, belief, and value change yet utilize behavioral tasks as homework assignments often designed to produce shifts in feedback from significant others.

Research into results of psychotherapy shows that all the therapeutic techniques mentioned above have proved effective on occasion and that no one method is superior to any other. The therapeutic quandary, of course, is when to use what technique. To some extent this decision will be affected by the treatment goal mutually agreed upon by client and worker (Chapter 9). Yet even the treatment goal does not automatically indicate appropriate techniques any more than does diagnostic understanding. It is the therapist's own need for vitalization that becomes the most critical ingredient in deciding upon techniques.

Vitalization possibility and subsequent strategies are preceded by probing activities. In the first interview, and often in the next few sessions, the therapist probes the client's manner of dealing with change efforts. Some clients will use their reason as a creative, searching tool for potential change. Others will use reason for defensive intellectualization and rationalization, self-preoccupation and excuses. When reason is available as a positive tool, the therapist is likely to make use of techniques associated with attitude change.

There will be clients who make constructive use of heightened awareness of feelings, sensations, and intuitions. Catharsis, emotional "explosions," and even quiet looking at aspects of here-and-now awareness will propel some people into new actions. On the other hand, the focus upon feelings can sometimes be as defensive a game as intellectualizing. Some clients will wallow in feelings, the way they have been doing for years. Techniques related to awareness change are used when probes reveal creative, working responses in these areas.

Similarly, there will be clients who relate positively to behavioral tasks while others see these as "superficial" and "failing to understand the depth of my problem."

Finally communication-feedback probes may be made by inviting significant others into the interview. There will be clients who are relieved and eager to involve their spouses or family members. Others will refuse further counseling if the therapist insists that significant others come in. If significant others are present the interaction may prove growth enhancing or it may prove stifling of engagement efforts.

These kinds of technique choices have often been linked with diagnostic categories; e.g., "With a compulsive you avoid techniques that encourage intellectualization." This linkage represents therapists' efforts to handle their own uncertainty by providing a kind of ready-made map or recipe. But diagnostic categories are not only unnecessary for this probing process but actually less objective. Diagnostic categories are never exacting in their effort to capture the dynamics of the person. The risk is that the therapist will end up treating the theoretical category rather than the client himself. Probes have the objective quality of making a hypothesis and then testing it out by therapeutic action and observing the results. Diagnostic categories are largely built upon untested assumptions and speculations, often derived from highly tainted data presented by the client at the start of treatment, when he is suspicious and self-protective and the therapist has little personal observation of the client to utilize in his assessment.

The strategy model has certain advantages over the other therapeutic models mentioned (insight givers, teachers, etc.). The strategist is primarily concerned with which approaches will most vitalize the interviews and are most likely to result in subjective or interpersonal engagement efforts. Some therapeutic roles encourage self-knowledge or insight as the principal achievement. As we have seen, even when reason is not used defensively it may be of only limited value if active S-O-S engagement is ignored or treated as secondary. Pursuit of the ideal of self-knowledge often results in reinforcing the self-alienation process by emphasizing ego self-speculation instead of active process engagement. Relation results from process engagement and is impaired by thinking that becomes self-stroking and self-preoccupation.

Another faulty ideal is the encouragement of self-actualization with the therapist commonly teaching as well as modeling "self-actualization" himself. For many people self-actualization can become a merry-go-round of sought-after peak experiences with considerable frustration, boredom, and despair in relation to most of their everyday living. Here the therapist-guru preaches a personality utopia just as his counterpart, the naïve revolutionary, preaches a social utopia. The quest for utopias inevitably ends in disillusionment, cynicism, rage, or despair.

Whenever the therapist models some ideals of "healthy functioning," whether this be self-understanding, self-actualization, being responsible, or demonstrating clear communication, there is the risk of sending the message: "Be like me." Clients endow therapists with gurulike wisdom anyway, so the risk of encouraging client conformity is strong. There is also the likelihood that the therapist-as-model is dangerously close to an exhibitionistic ego trip. Whenever a therapist's own ego inflation comes to the fore, he loses his detachment and is most susceptible to the client's control maneuvers.

Priority Considerations

Having reviewed the variety of ways of producing change as well as adapting technique to the creative responsiveness of the client, there still remains a question of what techniques are most likely to produce change efficiently and what techniques may tend to complicate, delay, or even inhibit the change process.

There is an applicable perspective that arises from many of the philosophical writings considered earlier: Krishnamurti, Castaneda, Pirsig, Ram Dass, and the Zen thinkers in general. Experiencing, awareness, creative response to the new, opening to the unknown of arising needs and potentials are ways of describing the growth process. This process is avoided, ignored, inhibited, and denied by rigidified role functioning maintained by an integrated set of beliefs, attitudes, assumptions, melodramas, and stereotypes. One must control others as well as one's own feelings and attitudes so as to play out those roles which will tyrannize, conform to, or seduce others into providing one with the needed happiness, however that might be defined. Herein lies one's justification for maintaining the set of rigid attitudes, avoidance mechanisms, and interpersonal games that are based upon catastrophic expectations and illusional hopes.

The shared perspective of the above writers suggests that the mind, the thought process itself, blocks growth. They suggest ways by which such thought process may be disrupted, shaken loose, and penetrated so that the individual may allow himself some new direct experiencing apart from his usual categorizations of his ''reality.'' Without reviewing their methods, which have already been described in earlier chapters, we can utilize their perspective as a means of evaluating the potential effectiveness of various psychotherapeutic techniques. We shall look first at two classes of contraindications of technique application:

1. If therapy is to open a client up to his own experience, then the therapist should avoid imposing his own perspective upon the client. This includes the therapist's prognosis of how far the client can or cannot go in his own growth effort. It also includes the therapist's teaching the client what beliefs are correct because they are "rational," or socially acceptable, or "humanistic," or "realistic." The therapist must avoid the role of placing new expectations upon the client to which the client must again conform, play out a new role to please the therapist, and continue to feel like an impotent victim rescued and directed by some powerful other person.

2. Therapists should discourage long-term therapy that places the client in a dependency role, whether this is for the purpose of "transference resolution," the accumulation of self-knowledge, or the ongoing collection of new "awareness experiences" aimed at a reformation of personality (the cure model). Not only do such long-term approaches needlessly delay the client's immediate engagement with his daily life situation, but they also promote the victim-guru relationship mentioned above. While long-term approaches are aimed at eventually dissolving this victim-guru relationship, they are inefficient and costly in their way of doing this and many times fail in this eventual goal anyway, perhaps partly because they have intensified the very problem they hoped to dissolve.

Let us look now at those techniques that have appeared to me most effective or efficient in producing change. These could be called the eclectic grouping of techniques compatible with the existential model.

1. The therapist will use reason to challenge, discredit, and ridicule those beliefs and attitudes used by the client to maintain the problem or symptom. His hidden grandiosity may be exposed, his catastrophic expectations will be challenged, his erroneous assumptions about the overwhelming power of his feelings and symptoms will be countered, his rigid definitions about

the type person he is and isn't will be questioned, his view of himself as helpless or angry victim will be called into question. Techniques discussed by Albert Ellis, Camilla Anderson, Viktor Frankl, Frank Farrelly, O. Hobart Mower, and Willard Mainord accomplish these ends. Assumptions about the meanings about behavior (one's own as well as others') may be relabeled as having potentially other meanings (Jay Haley, Paul Watzlawick). The therapist will also clarify possible directions, choices, need-meeting possibilities, and potential consequences of considered choices (William Glasser). The use of reason is a means of engaging the client's pragmatic self (defense-free ego) as a neutralizing force for the rigid melodramas of his security image. The therapist is moving the client toward a state of confusion or self-doubt concerning his growth-inhibiting attitude armor, which at the same time avails him of the possibility of new learning. Through such attitude unbalancing, the jostling therapist "throws" the client into the void of potential new experiencing.

2. The therapist will provide the client opportunities for new experiencing within the interview situation itself. He will promote awareness for the client both subjectively and interpersonally. This may occur through attending to feelings, sensations, fantasies, dreams, and resistances. Gestalt therapy provides a most direct route for such efforts. The therapist may seek to vitalize the interaction between a marital couple, among family members, or between himself and the client so as to break through rigidified control maneuvers (Carl Whitaker, Walter Kempler, Frank Farrelly, Everett Shostrom, Savlador Minuchin, Virginia Satir, Harold Greenwald, Sidney Jourard, Carl Rogers). The therapist may provide the client a new experience by the very nature of his attitude toward the client (negative provocation or affirming acceptance), by his capacity to give full listening-understanding attention (empathy) and by what he shares of his own experience with the client (transparency). New learning occurs, here, through the client's direct experience. Relaxation, hypnotic imagery and meditation may also be utilized as a means

of bypassing the usual mind sets of defensive attitudes so as to enable the client to allow a new way of experiencing himself. The client begins to discover his own source of power, his self-support, his emerging capacities, polarities, needs, his sense of growing individuation as a responsible meaning-maker. Such awareness-enhancing techniques will remain problem focused, in keeping with the short-term model of therapy. Whatever is learned by such experiences in the therapy session will be applied to his daily life situation through homework assignments.

3. New experiencing will be regularly encouraged in the client's daily living situation through the use of behavioral and interactional tasks given as homework assignments. More important than new experiences within the interview situation are these new experiences in the client's daily life process. It is here that the effectiveness of therapy is measured. It is here that the client's sense of autonomy, of self-adequacy is developed. The client may be asked to play with his life in an adventurous and experimental fashion. He will be asked to deal differently with his emotions, his symptoms, his significant others, his opportunities for trying out new potentials. Paradoxical tactics may be used in assigning tasks to break up the client's usual control maneuvers (Jay Haley, Paul Watzlawick, Viktor Frankl, Frank Farrelly, Milton Erickson). Behavior-modification techniques will prove useful. Albert Ellis, Salvador Minuchin, and William Glasser emphasize useful homework assignments that are cooperative rather than paradoxical in nature. Insights and new meanings will result from such experiences occurring between therapy sessions. These insights are the client's own and will be validated by his therapist as important new ideas that the client may wish to use in the future. As problems are resolved or the symptoms disappear the therapist is willing to let go of the client. He may wonder whether new symptoms have arisen within the client or his family as a means of further exploring a need for therapy, but if the client is comfortable with his new level of functioning he will not be pressured into continuing therapy by the "resistance" or "flight

into health'' therapeutic gambits. If he should require the services of the therapist in the future, the door is open.

Paradoxical Techniques

In the writings of Zen, Krishnamurti, Ram Dass, Castaneda, and est, there is a particular emphasis upon the use of paradox. Although paradoxical techniques were mentioned above, it may be useful to elaborate upon them here as these techniques have aroused considerable interest and controversy among professional helpers in recent years. Paradoxical techniques are frequently used by the eclectic strategist as they are in keeping with some key therapeutic aims. First of all, paradoxical strategies are likely to produce more rapid change than other techniques. Second, paradoxical strategies tend to bypass or even confuse the mind's efforts to problem-solve in patterned, ineffectual ways. Third, paradoxical strategies allow the therapist to remain in a more obviously detached position so that he is less likely to be hooked by the client's control maneuvers. The power struggle based upon ambivalence about change is largely avoided.

Paradoxical strategies have been described primarily by the gestalt therapists, the communication-task strategists (Haley, Erickson, Watzlawick), the logo-therapist Vitor Frankl, and Frank Farrelly.

Paradoxical techniques are so labeled because they tend to encourage the very symptom, troublesome feeling, pain, or problem that the client says he wants to stop. Figure 8-2 illustrates the strategy of a paradoxical technique.

In the left-hand diagram we see a common fault among inexperienced therapists. The client presents his emotional seesaw of ambivalence to the therapist ("I want to change/I fear changing"). The therapist supports the positive side of the ambivalence: "I'll help you. Why don't you try this?" The negative side of the ambivalence comes to the fore in the form of resistance as the client becomes fearful of what may happen if he changes. He

Figure 8.2

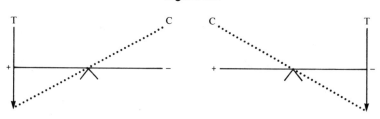

either rejects the suggestion or agrees to it but does not really invest himself in the effort.

On the other hand, when the therapist encourages the symptom, as in the right-hand figure, the client will often change in spite of himself. "You're holding back tears; fine, just give yourself a little lecture right now on why you shouldn't cry."

Why is it that paradoxical strategies are so effective? Usually resistance to change stems from a client's ambivalence about his problem. He is in clear conflict about changing and usually feels victimized by his symptom, which he blames for his inability to change. There are three dynamics that may come into play with paradoxical techniques.

First, the client is suddenly placed in a position where he is taking responsibility for his symptom rather than feeling victimized. For instance, a client is told that his depression is a useful, revealing experience and is asked to let himself become depressed—don't try to fight it—and pay attention to the thoughts that go on during depression (à la Ellis). The client's usual way of reacting to his depression is now confused. Instead of feeling sorry for himself or angry at himself he finds himself accepting the depression, owning it, validating it, yes—even wanting it! He is also getting clear acceptance and validation from the therapist: It's perfectly OK to have your symptom. The "let it be" message allows one a greater sense of freedom. One does not have to worry about fighting or pleasing a therapist.

A second dynamic is the fact that in validating the symptom one is affirming both sides of the conflict: "I want to beat my child, and that feeling is OK; I love my child and I don't want to hurt him, and that's OK too.'' When one can accept two sides of a conflict within oneself and see value in both sides, it is possible for a synthesis to occur—some third middle-ground possibility. "Being angry or disappointed in my child is sometimes a way of showing my love for him.'' As long as one is wedded to one side of the conflict and condemning the other side, one is stuck—righteous, guilty, immobilized.

The third dynamic in paradoxical strategy has to do with the manipulative quality of the symptom. Jay Haley has pointed out that symptoms are means of controlling others without taking responsibility for doing so.[1] The paradox forces the person into a position of either allowing the therapist to take control or else giving up the symptoms, in which case the therapist is again the winner, although the client has at least asserted her autonomy. For example, a woman with a reported compulsion to look in mirrors sought my help. She would check her appearance before going out of the house but found she was never satisfied and could not break away from the mirror for several minutes. She reported no other problems in the family. She was told to gather detailed data for the therapist in the following way. Any time she had the least desire to look in the mirror she should do so. She should allow herself to remain before the mirror until she could comfortably move away from it and not fight this experience. She was to write down the times when she began and when she ceased looking into the mirror. She was to let her husband know that this was a special task she must perform for her therapy. When she was seen two weeks later the symptoms had diminished in frequency and intensity. The task was continued for two more weeks. When next seen, the symptom was gone and she began to talk of frustration in the marriage that had never been mentioned initially. This then became the focus of treatment.

The most illuminating description of the use of paradox to be found in social work literature is the book *Provocative Therapy* by Frank Farrelly and Jeff Brandsma.[2] Farrelly's theory of practice and many case examples set forth how the therapist uses himself in a most active and engaging way in order to paradoxically unbalance the client's attitudes, symptoms, and problematic behavior. Here is an excellent description of what Harold Greenwald has also alluded to in his playful, vitalizing manner of relating to the defensive, manipulating ploys presented by clients.[3] Farrelly's contribution is particularly valuable to social workers, for his examples deal with a variety of highly resistive clients, not uncommon to social work caseloads.

By using surprise, humor, rapid-spontaneous feedback, exaggerated mimicry and ridicule Farrelly not only confuses defensive mind sets but also opens up a client's awareness of himself in disturbing ways. As he tries to deal with the fast-stepping, jestering, troublingly candid therapist, the client is immersed in combinations of chaos, self-doubt, anger, and laughter. Change occurs, paradoxically, in both attitude and behavior as the client seeks to prove the therapist wrong.

Here we have, then, a model for the eclectic use of treatment techniques that is consistent with the philosophical perspective developed earlier. As indicated previously, the creative responsiveness of the client to particular techniques is assessed in the early interviews and becomes an indicator for later therapeutic efforts. As we shall see in the next chapter, the particular goal agreed upon between the client and the therapist is another important factor affecting choices of technique. The three major areas of technique usage (attitude disruption, new experiencing within interviews, new experiencing outside interviews) remain the pillars upon which therapeutic change is built. How these technique areas are applied will be altered to a degree by client responsiveness and goals agreed upon.

The therapist is quite active in his use of the three technique areas described. From an analyst's perspective the existential therapist might appear too directive of the client's thinking and experiencing. The analytic model tends to leave every move, every choice to the decision of the client. While this is certainly an intense training in awareness and choosing, it is by no means the only route to such activities. The enormous amount of time commonly spent in analytic therapy for the resolution of ambivalences through experience of unconscious material is not only costly and dependency-inducing, but also unnecessary. A therapist can be quite active in challenging attitudes and values, in suggesting awareness, behavioral, and interpersonal tasks, yet still respect and affirm the client as a choosing person responsible for the meanings he creates from his experiences.

Notes

1. Jay Haley, *Strategies of Psychotherapy* (New York: Grune & Stratton, 1963), p. 17.

2. Frank Farrelly, *Provocative Therapy* (Madison, Wisconsin: Family, Social and Psychotherapy Service, 1974).

3. Harold Greenwald, "Play and Self Development," in Herbert A. Otto and John Man, eds., *Ways of Growth* (New York: Viking Press, 1968).

Chapter 9

The Client-Centered Commitment

The principle of client-centeredness has wide-ranging implications affecting diagnosis, prognosis, goal-setting, relating to interview themes, and termination. While many therapists would claim to be client-centered (social work has long espoused the adage, "Start where the client is"), the truth of the matter is that they are not. Instead they are either theory-centered or therapist-centered (therapist knows what's best, what's functional, what's mature). A great deal of effort is spent in trying to convince the client that change must come from him, but in reality most such effort is a controlling seduction, subtle parenting, or sometimes even a direct "I know best" message. This is not necessarily an indication of the therapist's own need, for some theories of therapy actually convey an absolute definition of pathology and prescriptions of change efforts for therapists to follow.

This subtle or overt authoritarianism runs counter to the existential idea that there is no model of how a person should live and that pathological life styles are just as valid as genuine expressions of humanity as are those defined as functional, healthy, or mature. The position here is that life, including human exis-

NOTE: This chapter is an updated and expanded version of Donald F. Krill, "A Framework for Determining Client Modifiability," *Social Casework,* 49, no. 10 (December 1968): 602–611. Used by permission of the Family Service Association of America.

tence in all forms, is perfect just the way it is. This does not mean
that it should not change. The very nature of life is that it will
change, like it or not. But the therapist has no need of his own to
change someone else so as to make him conform to some model
of the therapist's own. This view is quite contrary to the humanistic philosophy common among many helping professionals that
assumes they are an elite group whose destiny it is to cure the ills
of society and lead others to the good life.

The existential change strategist is committed to using his
skills to help others change and may even assert his own limits
about some type of change with which he will not become engaged. However, he is not linked to a model defining how others
should be, and he has no utopian hopes for reforming society.

For the existential change strategist, each client is his own
diagnostic formulation. No client fits into some abstractly constructed diagnostic category. The prognosis for change rests not
upon any diagnosis but rather upon the client's motivation and his
dialogue with the curious therapist seeking to understand the
person's life style and manner of thinking. The client's assertion
that he wishes to change in some radical or major way may be
looked upon as a setup for failure. The therapist deals with this,
however, not as an indication of the potentials or limitations of
the person but rather as a form of resistance to genuine therapeutic work.

Just as he dismisses the usual overemphasis on diagnosis and
prognosis, the existential strategist makes little of the termination
process. There is no set period of time that is required to "work
through" one's termination with therapy. Nor does the therapist
accept the role of deciding when the client is ready to terminate.
Termination arises quite naturally when nothing more is being
done in terms of therapeutic work. The therapist need not even
deal with this as resistance—the client tends to handle the issue
appropriately in terms of his own wants and needs when he
realizes the termination decision is fully his own at any time.

Too often the issue of termination, like that of prognosis, is an
expression of the therapist's bias as to how much a client should

change. This brings us to the matter f goals. Toward what end does the therapy proceed, and who decides this?

A therapist wedded to some single system of treatment is often likely to restrict the opportunities or possibilities for his client's therapeutic work. A therapist who holds self-understanding as his basic therapeutic model will dismiss as unmotivated many clients who may be quite responsive to some other therapeutic strategy.

It is quite possible, and highly realistic, to view goal possibilities from the perspective of the client himself. In doing so there are two useful factors to consider. First, how does the client view his problem and what are his hopes for change? Second, how does the client see change as occurring?

The therapist must then decide whether the appropriate helping methods are available, and also whether he as a therapist is willing to work with the client toward the end desired.

A black client may believe he can be helped only by a black therapist. An Indian, referred by his probation officer, may believe his only hope for change is through the tribal medicine man. A husband may be unwilling to deal with his marital conflict until he has first clarified his own needs through individual therapy. While the therapist may not automatically agree to such attitudes without further discussion, he will take them seriously and not assume them to be expressions of ''resistance.''

Goals of Client Modifiability

I have found a series of seven goal categories to be useful in allowing for variations in clients as they deal with issues of change.

1. provocative contact
2. sustaining relationship
3. specific behavioral (symptom) change
4. environmental change
5. relationship change

6. directional change (personalizing values)
7. insightful analysis

The framework is designed primarily for work with adult clients. It is applicable to family therapy and work with adolescents, but no attempt has been made to relate it specifically to work with young children.

The client in Category 1 (provocative contact) wants no help and will often make himself as unavailable as possible for any involvement in treatment and change. He remains set in his life style, despite its destructive aspects, because he believes no other life style is possible for him. Any therapeutic effort will have to be imposed upon this client in the hope of reaching him and kindling some awareness of the possibility for change.

The client in Category 2 (sustaining relationship) sees no hope for change in his circumstances or pain other than some relief of loneliness. He may have no significant others, or he may believe no change is possible in his relationships. His sole interest in therapy is in having a relationship with someone who is interested in and concerned about his plight. He does not seek understanding of the meaningful patterns of past or current relationships that have contributed to his problem.

The Category 3 (specific behavioral change) client is troubled by a specific behavior pattern or seeks help for symptom relief. He is concerned about a symptom, such as excessive drinking, sexual deviancy, phobia, depression, or hallucination, but is unable to relate it to other aspects of his life. He is otherwise satisfied with his performance or, at least, sees it as unchangeable. Focusing on past or current relationships and goals in life is meaningless to him and therefore ineffective.

The Category 4 (environmental change) client recognizes that his suffering is associated with forces in his environment. His distinguishing characteristic is the hope for change in something outside himself, even though this change may necessarily include inner changes. The client may have difficulty in his job or social milieu. He may feel oppressed or maligned by others having some power over him. Therapy is accordingly geared toward such change.

The Category 5 (relationship change) client is aware of the importance to him of significant others in his life—spouse, children, friends, parents. He is dissatisfied with some aspects of one or more of these relationships and wishes somehow to change and improve the relationship. He is able to see the connection between his own personal suffering and symptoms and the dysfunctional relationship.

The Category 6 (directional change) client's disturbance is often enmeshed in the problem of anomie. His sense of personal direction in life is either shaken or lacking; his values are confused, causing his choices to become vague, uncertain, and inhibited. His sense of freedom and responsibility is weakened, and his view of the future is often foreboding. Therapy therefore must be partly philosophical—the therapist helping the client understand basic realities of human existence and pointing him toward personalizing or else revitalizing a value system that is directly related to his concrete life situation of limits and opportunities. Directional change is also indicated in cases in which anomie apparently is not involved. The nature of the client's conflict and his way of responding to it may distort or cloud his view of reality, making clarification of his situation, values, and choices the obvious goal.

The Category 7 (insightful analysis) client wishes to undertake extensive personal analysis and is qualified to do so. His goal is to gain as complete an understanding of all aspects of his inner and outer functioning as possible through analysis of his expression, behavior, and associations. The category is included for the sake of completeness, although few clients may be so classified. Treatment should not be undertaken by a therapist who has not had extensive analytic training.

Two important qualifications underlie the use of the framework. One is the necessity of a careful assessment by study and dynamic understanding, so that the final determination of goal is a mutual decision. It is important to define mutuality; it is qualitatively different from acceptance of the client's stated goal as he sees his problems initially. The client's frequently stated objective—self-understanding in regard to the causes of the problem—is in most cases either a blind or an ignorant generalization. When carefully evaluated and tested, it may be seen to be one of the other treatment goals described above.

The other qualification is the changeability of a client's state of modifiability and, therefore, of the treatment goal. The judgment of category is made at a point in time. If the client were to seek help a year later, his state of modifiability might be quite different. Similarly, the category of modifiability may be changed in the course of treatment. If such change is not apparent to the client, the therapist may have to direct attention to it and its meaning in terms of a new treatment goal.

The categories of modifiability have no relation to an inferior–superior gradation of treatment goals. They are, in fact, based on a point of view that is in strenuous opposition to any such gradation, because the concept of gradation always exists in conjunction with a superior-system approach. There is no urgent need to lead a client from one goal to a "higher" one. Such a standpoint is contrary to the fundamental respect for the uniqueness of each client that is basic to the existential approach. Respect is also inherent in the therapist's willingness to work within the limits of the client's capacity to understand, seeing the mutually agreed-upon goal as equal in value to any other goal uniquely applicable to a client. Essentially, it is the application to therapy of the existential belief in and regard for an individual's uniqueness and personal freedom. As existence precedes essence, so the worth of an individual precedes the validity of any system that attempts to explain him. Cynicism and boredom are minimized for the therapist who appreciates the truth of such a view of human beings.

The proposed system may appear to be all-inclusive, viewing all clients as treatable or "workable" at some level. Obviously, some clients are unmotivated and ask for help simply as a means of manipulating a spouse, parent, probation officer, welfare worker, commanding officer, or prison warden. The essential significance of using this system is that the decision that a client is untreatable is made only after careful consideration of all categories of modifiability as possibilities.

The Treatment Goals

The seven goals may be further clarified by a discussion of the common characteristics of each as they appear in practice:

1. *Provocative contact* would include "backward" psychotics and severely retarded adults, psychotic or severely retarded children, "child-beating" parents, and "incorrigible criminals." In an effort to reach out to people such as these, people set in their life style usually because they believe no other to be possible, some form of "provocative contact" may be justified therepeutically. Behavioral-modification techniques, including the instigation of punishments and rewards, have been an effective way of working with these people. Through the lived-out experience of receiving punishments, or the threat of such, in the form of increasing discomfort in some concrete way, along with the satisfactions of sometimes being rewarded in pleasurable or kindly ways, the person is related to through his most primitive needs. There are serious dangers of misusing this category to "adjust" people to the values of society represented by the therapist and the institution. It should therefore be used with caution and only as a means of helping a person begin to experience himself as desiring (or concluding that he will continue to refuse) some other form of treatment goals; that is to say, his level of "modifiability" may shift to a different level of therapeutic readiness. The active confronting approaches of William Glasser and Frank Farrelly are also examples of effective therapeutic systems related to this category.

2. The basic ingredients for achieving a *sustaining relationship* are genuine interest and availability. Care, concern, and belief in the client's worthiness as a person, despite his failures

and limited circumstances, are basic to the therapist's healing responses. Although initial interviews may be fairly frequent, subsequent contact is often on an infrequent or "on call" basis. The therapist's availability by phone or personal contact is, nevertheless, critical in times of crisis. Often the clients may be shifted to some other helping person (a volunteer) or group in the community who can provide long-range contact.

With the sustaining relationship category, the therapist does not convey expectations of how the client should change his life in some manner. Yet at the same time he believes that in the very acceptance of the client's level of viewing himself and his world (as unchangeable, yet his needing someone to talk to who will try to understand and listen) there is the possibility of an affirming therapeutic contact, and from this the client may experience growth in some useful way. His growth may move him toward termination or toward a rising awareness of a new way of viewing his world, and how he might now somehow change it (a readiness for a new treatment goal).

3. For *specific behavioral (symptom) change,* treatment is aimed at bringing the symptom, or the effects of the symptom, under control in order to improve everyday functioning, which is otherwise impaired. The client's management of the symptom is dependent on his gaining knowledge and a new perspective of the symptom itself and its effect on functioning. Management may take the form of refusing a behavioral reaction despite feelings of compulsion (abstaining from alcohol); accepting the presence of a symptom (not becoming panicky when hallucinating or behaving as if his thinking is reality); or deliberately behaving contrary to the ordinary reaction to the symptom (working while depressed) or performing the very act that a phobia warns against. The unique approach in treatment is avoidance of discussion of the past or even of elaborate complaints in regard to the present. The goal is for therapist and client to work together on symptom control and any difficulties encountered in the process.

4. For *environmental change* the aim is to engage in forthright discussion of the particular troublesome area of activity and of reality-based action that may be taken to remedy the problem.

The problem may be in relation to job performance or the need for social relations or a creative outlet in life. It may be related to an occurrence that has affected the client's environment or his use of his environment, such as temporary illness, fatal disease, or the gain or loss of members of a household. Therapy is often short-term and may involve referral to another agency, such as a church, community center, employment office, or rehabilitation center.

5. Treatment for *relationship change* is aimed at symptoms or problems in relation to current meaningful relationships that are conflicted and are frustrating the client's own needs. Role failures, communication breakdown, interpersonal "games," and scapegoating are common areas of focus that reveal the nature of warped or distorted relationships. Variations and possibilities of this goal were dealt with in Chapter 7.

6. With directional change the overall objective in treatment is to clarify and personalize the client's own values, as they derive from the tasks and responsibilities inherent in his daily life situation. His sense of uniqueness develops as he turns his attention away from self-pity and toward his everyday life possibilities, activities, and limitations and makes decisions in accord with the values he has identified for himself within this context.

7. In *insightful analysis* the goal for the client is to uncover and understand his intrapsychic conflicts and to experience them in his relationship with the therapist so that they may be examined and clarified. An extensive understanding of the client's patterns of thought, feelings, and behavior is sought through frequent interviews over an extended period of time. Events of the past, dreams, associations, current relationships, and the interaction with the therapist provide the content of sessions.

It is important to distinguish between insightful analysis and the use of insight in seeking relationship change and directional change. When techniques that are uniquely appropriate to analysis are transposed to other therapeutic work, serious problems may arise. Such techniques include the nurturance of a neurotic transference relationship, the encouragement of ventilation and considerable insight in relation to early traumatic happenings, free association, and extensive attention to dreams and fantasies. Two antitherapeutic effects occur in the misapplication of the analytic model: The client's feeling of helplessness and impotence is encouraged rather than discouraged as he believes himself to be the victim of his unconscious and early traumas; and the client's ability to feel that his problems are unalterable on the basis of early happenings is enhanced. In addition, significant others are excluded from therapy, which can seriously limit or negate treatment results. The time element is also involved; the client delays doing much about the situation or crisis that brought him to seek help. Indeed, the postponements may go on not for weeks or months but for years! Finally, there is the very real controversy in regard to whether insight into early traumatic happenings is really the healing factor in analysis. If, as some believe, the factor of change is the intensive patient-therapist relationship and its resolution, insight therapy of an analytic nature once or twice a week would be a futile gesture in most cases, even by an analyst.

One must bear in mind that, when any of the seven designated goals is selected, it becomes the primary means of focusing treatment. Activity related to one designated goal may, however, be used as interview content for the purpose of achieving a different goal—the agreed-upon primary goal. For example, environmental change may be a subgoal in relation to the primary goal of directional change, relationship change, or insightful analysis. Obviously the primary goal in such cases is always more extensive than the temporary subgoal.

Goal–Technique–Mode Integration

The goal categories described suggest related therapeutic methods, as illustrated below:

1. Provocative contact: behavior modification, reality therapy, paradoxical strategies

2. Sustaining relationship: social work literature, Carl Rogers
3. Specific behavior (symptom) change: behavior modification, logotherapy, paradoxical strategies, drugs, hypnosis
4. Environmental change: social work literature, advocacy
5. Relationship change: family and marital therapies, paradoxical strategies, behavior modification
6. Directional change: reality, psychoanalytic, TA, gestalt, logo-therapy, rational-emotive, paradoxical strategies, non-directive
7. Insightful analysis: Freudian, Jungian, existential

There are so many therapeutic approaches in the current literature that the linkages described are merely suggestive and certainly not comprehensive.

As described in Chapter 8, treatment techniques are also chosen from a client-centered focus. It is not the diagnostic category that indicates the technique but rather the client's ability to work at change through his reason, his feelings, behavioral tasks, and the communication-feedback system of significant others. The same holds true for the goal category selected; there may be several therapeutic methods of working toward the same goal. The therapist probes to discover which will be most efficient and effective with a particular client.

In the preceding chapter we categorized effective techniques for change into three major areas: disruption of attitudes; experiencing the new within the interview; and experiencing the new through homework assignments outside the interview. Factors influencing the choice of techniques were the creative responsiveness of the client to varied ways of problem exploration as well as the goal of treatment.

The relation of goals to the three major technique areas becomes fairly obvious. Attitude disruption is a possibility with all goals described; however, it would be used less with the goals of sustaining relationship and environmental change. New experiencing during the therapy session is also possible with all goals but would be less of a factor with the goal of environmental change. The use of homework assignments for new experiencing would be applicable to all goals, but to a lesser degree with provocative contact and sustaining relationship goals.

In discussing the S-O-S perspective in Chapter 7 we saw a priority preference on the part of therapist for the mode of therapy used: communal, family, and marital approaches over group and individual where possible. Here again, however, the therapist's priority preference must be secondary to the uniqueness of the client's situation and personal view of change. Communal, family, and marital approaches are usually appropriate with the goals of relationship change and relationship-directional change.

The indicators for group or individual treatment modes described in Chapter 7 also tie in with the variations of goal categories. For example, with the goal of specific symtpom (behavior) change we commonly find the client not wanting to involve significant others, and significant others not seeing any need to be involved. The sustaining-relationship goal is commonly related to the client who lacks significant others in his present environment, or whose significant others refuse to engage themselves with the client's needs. The goal of directional change often indicates the need for the client to work out problems of his own identity related to value disintegration or confusion before engaging him with his S-O-S. With the categories of provocative contact and environmental change the client sees no personal problem and therefore often does not wish to have significant others involved in treatment.

On the other hand, it is sometimes possible and helpful to involve significant others in all of the goal categories described, particularly as an evaluative method for a more direct and comprehensive understanding of the client's problem and the appropriateness of his goal interest. The very involvement of significant others in the early assessment stage of treatment may reveal potentials or opportunities for change or help that were otherwise outside the client's and therapist's awareness.

The interactive complexity of goals, techniques, and modes of treatment may be further clarified by two case examples. It is particularly important to illustrate the idea that treatment can proceed quite effectively without any effort at clinical diagnosis. A dynamic understanding of the interplay of belief system, avoidance system, S-O-S, and wider influential systems (described in Chapter 7) remains essential. The eclectic use of treatment methods will be obvious.

Case Examples

A forty-year-old divorced woman sought help for family problems that involved all three of her children: Roberta, seventeen, who had been away from home at college for the past two months; Harry, sixteen; and Nancy, fourteen, the primary focus of concern because of her open rebellion against her mother. The mother had been divorced for two years, during which time she completed her Ph.D. and entered upon a demanding professional career. She had a boyfriend with whom she had been intensely involved over the past ten months. Her ex-husband had remarried and was living in a distant city.

Treatment has consisted of seventeen interviews with the mother, the first and seventeenth sessions involving the whole family, the eighth session involving Nancy and mother, and the fourteenth with the mother's boyfriend. The other thirteen sessions were with the mother alone. Her boyfriend was also seen for four individual sessions. Treatment has thus far lasted ten months. Sessions were one and a half hours in length and were held every two or three weeks. The family lived out of state, and the distance as well as the mother's job demands made more frequent contacts quite difficult.

The initial family session resulted in considerable expression of anger and tears on the part of all three children toward their mother. They felt she had little interest, care, or concern for them because of her "selfish" involvement with her work and her boyfriend, whom they disliked. They felt she used them to do household chores that did not interest her. They also saw her as critical and inconsistent in relation to discipline—she was overly critical and restrictive when she was at home, but when she was gone during the evening or overnight (sometimes because of job demands and sometimes because of the boyfriend) there was no supervision over the children whatsoever. Mother's major concern was Nancy's staying out all night on occasion, going around with a "rough" crowd, and chain-smoking.

The mother appeared aloof, intellectual, and defensive during this session. After an hour I dismissed the children and talked to the mother alone. I summed up the children's complaints as their feeling they must give to her but get little in return. Their rebellion against her restrictions appeared to be an expression of this resentment. Since the mother had raised the question of placing Nancy, or both Harry and Nancy, with their real father, I emphasized that the mother would need to look at the question of whether she wanted the intense mother role with her children or not. Perhaps she would be happier without them living with her. She wanted to explore this, so I suggested three tasks for her following the first session.

The first task was for her to be home each night, or have an adult sitter there if she could not be home herself. She should do this for at least a month. Second, she was to reduce the number of overnights she was spending with her boyfriend, away from her home. Third, if she wanted to explore her mother role, she should spend less time on her professional work when she was at home. It would be important for her to talk to each child separately about rules and expectations and find some point where she could give each child somewhat more leeway on a previous restriction. If she set a rule, she needed to follow up carefully to see if it had been obeyed or not. She needed to seek opportunities to relate to her children apart from disciplinary concerns.

Let us examine the treatment plan for this client. First, the important factors in dynamic understanding were belief system, avoidance system, S-O-S system, and wider systems of influence. The mother saw herself as bright, professionally capable, attractive, and independent. She expressed both ambivalence and guilt about her role as a mother. She realized she was often preoccuped more with her own needs than with the needs of the children. Yet she believed she had given them considerable emotional support in past years, and, since the divorce, she needed to use her energies in other ways in order to survive with some sense of self-satisfaction.

She tended to avoid her own feelings of weakness, self-doubt, and need for love as these did not integrate well with her image of independence. She could be easily angered when such feelings displayed themselves in the children, and she would tell them the same thing she told herself: Be strong, handle it yourself. On the other hand, her feelings around dependence and weaknesses would sometimes break through in exaggerated demands toward both her boyfriend and her ex-husband. She experienced the recurring split within herself between independence and dependence as an identity crisis. She feared losing both the children and her boyfriend, yet worried about losing her own precarious sense of autonomy if she conformed to their expectations.

The three children were already engaged in the process of emancipation from the family—the younger two handling this stage of development somewhat prematurely in reaction to the mother's withdrawal from them since the separation from their father. The remarried father remained available for visits by the children on a regular basis, at least monthly. He was willing to have the children live with him; however, this was apparently an uncertain stance since the children did not feel fully accepted by his second wife.

The mother's present boyfriend was intensely involved with her, yet expressed clear uncertainty about any marital commitment. Whenever she became emotionally upset in relation to her own sense of insecurity and neediness, he would withdraw and take a parentlike comforting stance. He avoided dealing openly with his own fears of a long-term, live-in commitment. If, on the other hand, the mother threatened to drop the lover relationship, he would become depressed.

The mother's job was demanding. She had an administrative

position with a governmental project, which required frequent travel. While this job was professionally satisfying and empowering for mother, the very nature of the work encompassed recurring demands, heavy responsibilities, and a never ending series of expanding opportunities for development. To handle such a position with professional satisfaction required of the mother considerable time and effort, often invading her evenings and weekends. On the other hand, such a job provided her with a realistic rationalization for her lack of time and energy for the children. She could see that her own high standards affected the manner in which she performed in her work.

From this dynamic framework, let us look at the therapeutic treatment plan concluded. The goal decided upon was relationship-directional change, since mother's problem awareness and concern encompassed her own identity as well as her relationship with children, boyfriend, and ex-husband. The mode of therapy was a combination of joint sessions involving the children, and later the boyfriend, as well as individual sessions. The mother would be seen individually as a means of helping her decide her own direction as mother, lover, and professional. Joint sessions focused upon significant-other interactions so as to test out her efforts in new directions. The joint sessions provided the therapist with both access and an opportunity to utilize the children and boyfriend in a manner that enhanced change as rapidly as possible.

The choice of techniques varied in accordance with mother's interest and response to probing efforts. Behavioral tasks were used initially to help the mother engage herself directly with the question of whether or not she wanted to maintain and enhance the parental role. It appeared to me that the use of historical exploration and insight efforts at the outset would only promote the client's own shaky self-confidence and play into her efforts to intellectualize and rationalize about her ambivalent attitudes. The most rapid way to strengthen her confidence, as well as to promote trust in the therapeutic relationship, appeared to be that of moving the mother toward a decision she could activate.

Techniques dealing with awareness, attitudes, behavior, and communication feedback were all possibilities with this woman. Techniques were selected in response to her manner of working. Paradoxical techniques were used whenever possible in order to sidestep resistance, promote self-acceptance, and encourage new efforts. Such tactics brought about quick results in the elimination of headaches, the heightening of awareness, the expression of feelings of anger and weakness, and the acceptance of her own needs in situations where others were demanding that she neglect herself and attend to them.

Techniques aimed at new experiencing within the interview itself were the mainstay of most therapy interviews: the caring interest and affirmation of the therapist; the quiet, empathic acceptance and understanding of mother's turmoil; the sharing of personal feelings and experiences of the therapist as they related to situations discussed; and the encouragement of present feeling and sensation awareness.

Techniques aimed at attitude disruption were used on occasion when the mother was less upset and therefore capable of a working use of her intellect. She explored some cause–effect connections that appeared to be patterns spanning relationships with her parents, her husband, her parenting methods, her attitudes about work, and her efforts with her boyfriend. She also developed some personal insights in response to behavioral efforts she had made and the feedback from others that had occurred. These behavioral efforts were examples of homework assignments aimed at new experiencing and resulted from the clarification of choices and commitment to new plans for action.

The span of techniques possible for this client suggests an important therapeutic challenge. In any given interview, how does the therapist decide which techniques he will use and when? The following chapter will deal with the question of how both scientific and artistic components of therapeutic responsibility came into play in his timing of technique utilization.

Let us return now to the flow of treatment action.

The first two sessions focused upon the children, but the

client's sense of competence as a mother grew rapidly in response to the successful use of the tasks with her children. Occasionally she would bring up parenting issues in later interviews, and in the eighth session she brought Nancy along because of a crisis involving a shoplifting incident. But for the most part, from the third session on the mother concentrated upon herself and particularly her wants related to her job and boyfriend.

She saw her underlying fears as primarily related to the insecurity of the boyfriend relationship. He did not want to marry her, and she was not sure when he might decide suddenly to move out of the state to a different job, as he had spoken of doing on occassion. At the same time she was reluctant to involve herself with other men for fear her boyfriend would become jealous and leave her. This ambivalence was dealt with primarily with gestalt and reality-assessment techniques, which involved her exploring the roots of some of her attitudes in her family of origin. The matter of dealing with her own parents also took the form of a homework assignment to be done on a visit to her parents. She was to clarify her own lifestyle stance to them instead of hiding or disguising it, as she had been doing.

By the tenth session she had concluded that she must expand her own adult relationships—with both women and men—and that the accomplishment of this would even have a constructive effect upon her children. She had her first date with a new man since she had begun seeing her boyfriend fifteen months before. Her continued dating resulted in the inevitable crisis with the boyfriend, and it was during this period that he too became involved in treatment. He had become extremely depressed and agitated, claiming now that he had been on the verge of asking her to marry him.

The mother continued to date the new man and found herself both free and comfortable in this relationship. She and her boyfriend went through agonized, ambivalent discussions together and finally terminated their relationship, both feeling it was probably an inevitable ending.

Following the resolution of the boyfriend relationship, the

mother began to focus upon arising concerns about management of her children. Her own conflicts about control and authority came to the fore, and the two younger children were more actively resisting the mother's control efforts. This resulted in the family interview of the seventeenth session, where the focus was upon the needs and tasks related to the emancipation process.

The second case example also involves family problems, but the client's view of change was almost the polar opposite of the first example. A forty-year-old working mother of five children came to me for help with what appeared an overwhelming abundance of problems. She had a sixteen-year-old son who was out of her control. She had signed a note so he could get a car, and now he had quit his part-time job and was threatening to quit school. He was in constant conflict with his stepfather, and she felt she had to defend and support the boy, yet at the same time she realized she was babying him. The stepfather, her present husband, worked as a salesman but seldom brought in any money because he claimed he had to learn his new line of sales, and this might take a year or two. They lived on the mother's income from teaching kindergarten. She argued with him constantly because of his authoritarian, insensitive attitude toward her and the children. Occasionally he beat her. He was also seductive with the five-year-old girl, who was the only child of their marriage. The husband and wife never had sexual relations any more and slept separately. She had been seriously considering divorce for some time and threatened it on occasion. In addition to this, there were other family demands. The maternal grandmother lived nearby and had recently been in the hospital and now needed my client's care and attention. An older daughter who had married when she became pregnant had recently left her husband and returned home to her mother. Another daughter living in Oregon had recently reported that she was pregnant and would soon marry. My client further had trouble keeping her attention on her work, complained of some depression and of being overweight (about 50 pounds).

During the course of a year's work with this woman, at first in weekly interviews and later half-hour sessions on alternate weeks so that she could afford the private fee, changes did occur. Although the boy quit school, he did later acquire a job, which he held, and planned to return to school soon. All of the children in the family seemed under better disciplinary control. The daughter who had returned home because of marriage problems went back to her husband at the mother's insistence. The grandmother began managing on her own quite well. The husband brought home more money and changed sales jobs—apparently for the better. However, my client still had marital conflicts, cycles of depression, and the problem with overweight.

I tested out various approaches to her problem during the initial phase of treatment: focus on the relationship with her son, or husband, or mother; focus on what her own needs seemed to be, aiming for some clarification of direction in her life; focus on her symptom of overweight. Soon it became apparent that this woman was not wanting to work therapeutically at any of these goals. She would make efforts and then report failure, or else first report success and then failure by the next session. What soon emerged was her utter sense of ugliness and inadequacy and her expectation of being criticized, rejected, and dropped from treatment because of disappointing my expectations. Even efforts to confront her with such transference patterns met with no success. She had been in therapy a couple of years prior to seeing me and reported how that therapist had finally given up in despair with her.

Once I realized this (and it took about twelve sessions before this primary problem of expected rejection seemed clear), I worked with her thereafter with the goal of sustaining relationship and in so doing provided her with the one thing she desired out of therapy—someone who would listen and care no matter how often she failed and how overwhelming life sometimes became for her. She wanted someone who would understand, yet not be overwhelmed himself by her problems.

The positive changes mentioned earlier occurred, I am convinced, not because we worked at them as problems periodically (which we did), but rather because she was able to operate more realistically and consistently once she felt rooted and secure in a relationship that sustained her. This was accomplished in a relationship where change was not required or even expected, although it was accepted as valid when it occurred. Certainly the force of paradox was also at work in the therapist's stance: no need to change!

This second case example will not be evaluated in detail according to dynamics and treatment planning. It was used to illustrate a way of working with a client very different from the first example. In the second case the interrelationship between the woman's sense of inadequacy and fear of failure, her multiple realistic problems, and the goal of sustaining relationship is fairly obvious. The mode of individual treatment was used because of the mother's refusal to involve any significant others, fearing that their presence would only make matters worse. The techniques this woman was most responsive to were those of experiencing the new within the interview itself—empathy, caring, and a non-demanding, paradoxical attitude on the part of the therapist. When techniques for heightening awareness, for rational insight or for behavioral tasks were offered as probes they were to no avail.

In this chapter and the one preceding we have explored the existential treatment principles of experiential change emphasis and a client-centered orientation. We see their interrelationship in considering dynamics, mode, goal choice, and techniques. A third principle is also intertwined with these treatment activities. This is the personal engagement of the therapist that demonstrates and deals with his values, feelings, and attitudes. This principle will be explored in the next chapter.

Chapter 10

The Therapist's Use of Self

We have seen the utility of an existential perspective through our focus upon client-centeredness and experiential process engagement. This perspective relates to the varied aspects of therapy: diagnosis, dynamic understanding, prognosis, goals, modes, technique selection, and termination. In all these areas the concern is for the client's understanding and change. There is another important existential principle, which has to do with the therapist's focus upon himself, his use of his own subjectivity, his personal feelings, sensations, intuition, value responses during the counseling process. This is the artistic part of therapy.

In Chapter 8 we saw the relationship between the use of technique and the vitalization of the interview situation. Vitalization is the way the therapist experiences process engagement on the part of the client. The lack of such engagement results in boredom of therapist and client and the encouragement of continued alienation. The principle of experiential process engagement emphasizes the eclectic use of techniques by the therapist in order to get something new to happen. The principle of client-centeredness suggests ways of evaluating the client's perspective and situation so as to expedite process engagement possibilities. The client is met as a responsible, choosing person rather than as a conforming patient. The third principle deals with how the therapist uses himself in order to promote process engagement.

While his role is that of a spontaneous strategist, his manner is humanly revealing. How, then, does the therapist utilize his own subjective process as a means of dialogical engagement?

The interplay of knowledge (what is already known) and creative expression (the spontaneous emergence of the new) has been illustrated in dramatic form in Robert Pirsig's book *Zen and the Art of Motorcycle Maintenance*. He deals with the interplay of science and art, of knowledge and intuition, of the world of categorized dichotomies and the world of unknown wisdoms.[1] His notion of "Quality" (no-mind, direct experiencing, pure awareness without object, creative openness and readiness) can be transferred from motorcycle maintenance to therapeutic problem solving as shown in Figure 10-1.

Figure 10.1

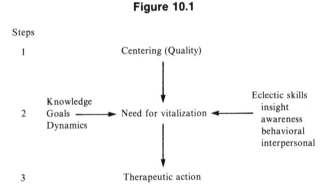

Figure 10-1 shows three steps in the creative process of therapeutic work, whether social action, community organization social-work activity, or psychotherapy. Step one has to do with the therapist's own subjective condition—his creative readiness. Step two includes all the matters of knowledge discussed in the previous three chapters—modes, goals, techniques, and so forth. Step three is the resulting helping action that is not so much chosen but rather emerges with a clarity and certainty. It is like the notion of Samurai swordplay and archery mentioned earlier. The correct action flows by itself.

An essential ingredient of this activity is the therapist's personal need for vitalization, which has been emphasized by Harold Greenwald, a psychoanalyst, and Carl Whitaker, a family therapist.[2] Greenwald coyly describes his approach as "play therapy with adults," and Whitaker labels himself an "existential family therapist." Neither conceptualizes his work as I shall describe it here. Both state, rather, that it is their intent to enjoy the therapeutic interview. Both come to a client system with considerable knowledge and skill variety. Both seek a vitalization of the interview situation as much for their own satisfaction as for that of the client.

Relating this model to psychotherapy, in the first few client interviews the therapist seeks a knowledgeable understanding of the problem in terms of psychodynamics and interpersonal dynamics through techniques to see how the client responds to various approaches—exploration of history, current attitudes, and emotions, dealing with interpersonal situations, and behavioral tasks. The nature of the treatment goal will suggest which techniques will probably be tried first. For instance, if the goal is improved marital communication, one would be tempted to begin by having both partners present and using interpersonal techniques that will reveal and begin to test out the way the two people interact. This early exploration provides the basic knowledge framework and sense of technique effectiveness that will undergird ongoing therapy.

Once this groundwork is laid, the centering-vitalization-action model comes into play. At the beginning of any session, the therapist "centers" himself. He seeks a state of mind where nothing is going on inside himself. He opens himself up to the "quality" (in Pirsig's term) of the situation addressing him. This is much like empathy, in that the therapist attunes himself completely to the client—what he sees, hears, smells, and feels in relation to the person or persons before him. This might also be described as primordial experiencing. He enters that unknown place of the creative process itself. The poet, the artist, the musician, the mystic are all familiar with this experience. Then, while in this totally open, responsive state of mind, the therapist begins to experience a need for vitality, for something new to emerge—either between himself and the client or among the clients. This is the point of intuitive interplay between his knowledge, technique, skills, and the live situation of which he is now a part.

The result is a certainty of therapeutic action to which he gives expression. This might involve the use of insight, awareness, interpersonal maneuvers, or behavioral strategies. He may assume any of the therapeutic roles (insight giver, teacher, model), or even some combination of these. But he is not acting. He is fully himself. There may be times, later in the interview, where he repeats the centering process as one theme is concluded and another is about to arise.

The therapist's best preparation for an interview is to review his knowledge of the client in relation to the last interview. In doing this, he may postulate potential strategies. This provides him with a kind of mindset, but not a plan, for the forthcoming interview. He then "loses his mind" in the centering process in order to discover the uniqueness of today's situation. This centering-vitalization-action process may occur within a few moments or may take considerable time.

Centering is a process of inner quiet, inner waiting. The centering frame of mind does not render the therapist a silent, passive blob at the start of each hour. He may still interact with the client while in this centered state. However, he is coming, inside himself, from a place of no intention, no direction. The certainty with which the therapist eventually proceeds does not give him a sense of absolute truth about his activity. He continues to be responsive to the reactions of the client as they engage each other.

The centering process is not only for the purpose of empathy, affirmation, and acceptance; it is also the "fertile void" out of which therapeutic action grows. One not only contacts the client in as empathetic, engaging a way as possible; one is also attuned to a gestalt-like arousal within oneself. This is the vitalization and finally certainty of action of steps two and three.

Ram Dass emphasizes that the most important therapeutic activity is the therapist's ability to "center" himself, to be detached from his own ego preoccupations. Such centering gives the client the experience of "having room to be himself." The major work for the therapist, according to Ram Dass, is the inner effort at centering.[3] Once this is achieved, therapy flows naturally, with the therapist using his knowledge and skills appropriately and successfully avoiding the "hooks" or control maneuvers set up by the client.

Similar to Pirsig's "Quality" is Joseph Chilton Pearce's "Continuum of Possibilities." In his *Exploring the Crack in the Cosmic Egg,* Pearce points out that both Jesus and Don Juan reveal the same truth about life. In order to engage oneself creatively with life (the sole point of it all), one must break out of one's culturally determined "reality" identities, perceptions, and conceptualizations. The "continuum of possibilities" is the process of experiencing the here and now apart from any conceptualization. This amounts to a state of readiness for engagement in a given situation that is completely unbiased by what one has known before. One will make use of previous knowledge and experience in the act itself. But to participate in the creative process is to make oneself available to unknown possibilities.[4] Such is the activity of centering.

The satisfaction for the therapist as spontaneous strategist is in the vitalization of the creative process of living—and in therapy this means engagement with the client in change activity. The nature of such satisfaction is interactive as opposed to role-fulfilling. One is not gaining primary satisfaction as authority, as caring parent, as teacher, as understanding helper. Satisfaction comes from engaging with the client in relation to change. Vitalization toward change is the therapist's creative act. It is discovered, like other creative art forms, in the realm of the unknown.

No person can comfortably tell another what technique to use and when. The choice of technique emerges from the therapist as an integrated person. One can learn knowledge (dynamic understanding, interpersonal system functioning, goal possibilities, and techniques) from a teacher or supervisor. Skills must be developed by the painful process of trial and error. One cannot expect a sound inner integration without first having gained both knowledge and technique experience. In order to acquire such experience, one must often behave in a somewhat stilted, mechanical, uncomfortable fashion. Techniques will sometimes fail because of this very discomfort, and this needs to be understood as part of the learning process itself.

The artistic and scientific compotents of the therapist's use of himself are of equal importance. An imbalance of these factors can be as much a problem for professional social workers as it is for students. The technician who neglects his own artistic development tends toward dehumanizing clients in an already alienated society. On the other hand, when the therapist is on his own "ego trip" of "helping" and is ignoring the scientific scope of his work, he is behaving irresponsibly toward those who seek to trust him.

The centering-vitalization-action model lends itself to an eclectic use of treatment techniques. An imbalance in either the scientific or the artistic side tends to wed a therapist to a single therapeutic system in a dogmatic fashion.

Interference and Humiliation

In Chapter 5 we examined a way of human functioning stemming from process identity that focused upon the interplay of no-mind and pragmatic-self mental states. The centering-vitalization-action model is an expression of this behavior in the helping role. Earlier we looked at how this natural process of no-mind and pragmatic-self interplay is often impeded by arousal of security-image and panic-apathy-rage states of mind. This same experience is a common occurrence in therapeutic activity when affirming interest is impeded by a therapist's self-preoccupations and negative emotions. When such troubling reactions arise for the therapist and are dealt with by hiding, repression, self-speculation, or blame the result is heightened alienation or distancing in the client-worker relationship. It is therefore important to understand how the therapist can remain engaged with his client by actively using his own negative, threatening subjective reactions. Engagement through risk of humiliation is his most direct route for avoiding alienation.

Carl Rogers dealt thoughtfully with this therapeutic dilemma by emphasizing the therapist's inner need for a positive acceptance and affirmation of the client. When this state of mind, described as empathetic understanding, was interfered with by the therapist's arising feelings (anger, suspicion, seductive desire, boredom, anxiety, despair), Rogers stated that it was important for the therapist to give expression to such personal responses.[5] This therapist "transparency" became even more strongly emphasized in the encounter group movement. It was clearly a departure from the previous idea that the therapist should remain aloof, detached, and objective so as not to let his personal feelings interfere with the therapeutic process.

The concept of countertransference combined with unrealistic assumptions about client fragility have resulted in exaggerated concerns about therapist self-disclosure. As Rogers says, when a strong emotional response within the therapist impairs his honesty and directness with a client this issue must be addressed. Whether this be countertransference (a neurotic, unrealistic reaction to the therapist) or whether it be a realistic, appropriate response to the behavior, attitude, or appearance of the client makes little difference. The point is that the therapist needs to find some way of dealing with his response that will be constructive rather than destructive to the client. The tendency to hide such subjective reactions from the client tends to be as destructive as ill-considered ways of expressing them.

The emphasis upon therapeutic transparency by such writers as Rogers, Jourard, Greenwald, Whitaker, Kempler, Durkin, Burton, Farrelly, Glasser, and Mowrer provides an answer to the therapist's dilemma of negative subjectivity interference. To bypass the potential alienation of his own negative responses he must be willing to risk exposure of even his own fears, greeds, pettiness, and erroneous judgments. It might be speculated that loneliness, despair, boredom, angry controlling maneuvers, and even suicide on the part of therapists are related to their personal refusal to bring their own personal responses into the interview spotlight. The therapist must be willing to share fantasies, dreams, feelings, sensations, intuitions, and values that can become strong interfering preoccupations.

As we saw in Chapter 5, the movement from alienation to no-mind/pragmatic-self activity will often require humiliation—the exposure and disillusionment of security-image control efforts. While it is often unnecessary to encourage clients to pursue such a painful activity, the therapist himself utilizes this action where possible. It is part of his discipline for being an effective therapist. The centering-vitalization-action model seldom occurs when the therapist's own ego strivings are in the way.

What of the client's reaction to such direct exposures? Can the client handle it? Isn't this unfair and neglectful of the needs and readiness of the client?

The principle of client-centeredness again takes priority. There will be situations in which such therapist exposure is inconsistent with the goal of therapy. There may be occasions when the therapist must contain his own subjective reaction. Generally speaking, however, exposure is more the therapist's problem than the client's. The therapist rationalizes his way out of exposure "for the good of the client." In most circumstances clients are probably relieved rather than profoundly threatened to observe the humanness of their therapist.

Walter Kempler, in his book *Gestalt Family Therapy,* clearly explains the humiliation component often involved in therapeutic transparency. He points out that therapists tend to have difficulty sharing their frustrations openly with clients because they are hesitant to reveal the whole truth of the matter. Related to a frustration is a hidden fear (''you're boring me and I'm afraid you won't like me if I say so''), and related to the fear is also a hidden wish (''I want you to believe that I am an interested, helpful therapist'').[6] The ''revealing'' therapist tends to reveal the frustration, but not the fear and wish behind it. Without the full message, such revelations tend to sound like attacks and threaten to distance the relationship. It is the humiliating aspect of the message that is left out, and the result is alienation rather than reconciliation.

Variations of Transparency

The therapist can lay the groundwork for exposure by promoting a personal, friendly openness about himself from the very start. There are numerous forms of personal transparencies that are nonthreatening and set the atmosphere for openness. The therapist may share his positive feelings and sensations. He may share negative moods that are unrelated to the client—fatigue or irritability that was present even before the session began. He may share personal experiences that are related to the client's situation—sometimes aspects of his own life such as his family, hobbies, likes, and dislikes, and sometimes his problems and how he dealt with them. He may share some of his own present patterns of behavior, feelings, or attitudes that could potentially arise within the therapeutic setting as interfering factors. Here he is warning and even inviting the client to engage him when he is being nontherapeutic. ''I sometimes tend to lecture, to talk too much, when I'm really feeling unsure of myself. Feel free to remind me of this or even ask me about it if you sense this to be happening. I try to control it but I'm not always successful.''

Spontaneous humor is one of the most valuable expressions of a therapist. To catch the funny edge, the absurdity of either a client's idea or one's own and be able to reveal this with laughter can have amazing results in shifting a client's perspective from self-pity to self-transcendence. To sing out with "nobody loves me; everybody hates me; think I'll go out and eat worms!" can counteract both the therapist's mounting ennui and the client's misery and self-castigation.

A most important form of personal transparency is the therapist's sharing of his own values, and this may even involve religious or philosophical beliefs. There is a difference between "laying on of values" and sharing one's own beliefs as simply one's own. This can be emphasized by expressing openly to the client that others hold contrary value positions: "To each his own, but this is where I am on the subject."

At times the therapist will set forth his personal values as a means of clarifying or challenging a value issue raised by the client. He may, for instance, assert that there is value in suffering, that disillusionment is often necessary before growth can occur, that suffering such as anxiety, guilt, boredom, and resentment are indications of pursuing change, or (like Frankl) that the very endurance of unchangeable suffering can be an ennobling experience. He may assert his own belief in freedom of choice, challenging deterministic attitudes that are rationalizing the client's view of his own helplessness. He may emphasize the importance of affirming, dialogical relationships with significant others and point out the interdependence of responsibility, trust, and commitment as the necessary undergirding of such relationships.[7]

There are times when the therapist will assert a value position in response to a request or challenge by the client. This sometimes occurs when the therapist is unwilling to contract a goal for change posed by the client. A parent may insist that the therapist see his young child for individual therapy without parental involvement. The therapist may refuse on the basis that he sees the child not as the only problem but rather as expressing problems of the family.

If the therapist has no absolute value framework and reveres the unique world view of each client, then how can he assert his value position? Let us take the example of a suicide threat. There are several possible reactions to such a threat:

1. clarifying the client's personal responsibility for the potential act and pointing out possible consequences
2. affirming the potential act as possibly a legitimate decision and suggesting a discussion of arrangements—how the act might best be accomplished, getting one's effects in order, etc.
3. encouraging exploration of (validating) the mental state, desperation or despair, related to the suicidal wish, but putting off the act
4. heightening the client's awareness of his ambivalence related to the act, exploring both sides so as to move toward a possible synthesis and altered decision
5. taking immediate action to prevent the suicide, such as hospitalization or forceful restraint.

Each of these responses is a correct (or incorrect) response in relation to a specific therapist-client interchange. The therapist is not coming from a position that says suicide is right or wrong. Suicide is suicide. The only absolute is that life in all its forms is in some way a perfect expression in and of itself. Value assertion is always a relative viewpoint that arises from a given situation. "Here I stand as a person" is the therapist's message, which is different from "This is what you should or should not do." If the therapist restrains a violent action it is on the basis of his own creative response to that given situation. It is in no way an assertion of what is ultimately right or wrong. What would have happened in human history if Judas had been talked out of betraying Christ? Judas himself followed the betrayal with suicide, but was his act of either betrayal or suicide ultimately bad? The Bible had prophesied the betrayal as necessary long before it took place. The value assertion by a therapist operates in the same way as other therapeutic actions as set forth in the centering-vitalization-action model. The therapist knows with certainty his own best response to a client situation. This is not like Fletcher's "situation ethics," which is based upon a reasoned assessment of the situation. The ethical decision emerges as a naturally arising gestalt.

The value issue is certainly complex and again must take into consideration the client's own level of valuing. In his book *The Destiny of Man,* Nicholas Berdyaev, the Russian existentialist, defines three levels of ethics: the ethics of law, the ethics of redemption, the ethics of creativity.[8] Translating his categorizations into psychological terminology, we might call these the three valuing levels of social adjustment, affirming acceptance, and realizing one's authentic self. The therapist is able to understand the valuing process at all three levels and will gear his own use of values to the level of the client's need.

The therapist will sometimes come from a value assertion of social adjustment. This generally occurs when there is no clear commitment by the client to work on his problems, at least as they relate to some antisocial act being threatened (whether suicide, homocide, child beating, or other serious crimes). The therapist has in some way been involved in the situation with the client—by referral or even as the issue arises in the midst of an already existent helping relationship. As a responding member of the situation the therapist asserts his position: "I cannot let you do this. Whether it is good or bad for you to do what you propose, I don't know. I can only say that I disagree and since I am a part of this now, this is what I must do."

In this example, is the worker an extension of society's laws and values? In a sense he is, insofar as he has been influenced by his society. He is also acting as an influencing member of his society as he deals with a client. Yet he also recognizes and conveys the relativity of his personal value position. Here he departs from a legalistic ethic which asserts, "That act is wrong, bad or evil." The client has the person of the therapist to deal with, not the law itself. The therapist is neither libertarian (do your own thing) nor authoritarian (it is right or wrong to do this).

A second value stance often assumed by the therapist is that of affirming acceptance. This is the "you're OK" or "it's OK" position. In religious terms it would be an assertion of the activity of grace and forgiveness: "You are loved or accepted in spite of the fact that you think you shouldn't be." While the therapist is not a purveyor of grace like the priest, minister, or rabbi, he can assert a similar position that is fully personal and human.

Another form of affirming acceptance is the attitude of the therapist toward the circumstances of the suffering client. This may be similar to "divine will" in religious thinking.

Case Examples

A thirty-year-old businessman was seeing me because he was frightened by his own rageful impulses toward his only daughter. The six-year-old girl was severely handicapped by cerebral palsy. The father was tortured by the prospect of her ongoing disability and the burden it placed upon both him and his wife. Although a Catholic, he had sought help from a fundamentalist church group, which had assured him that his daughter could be healed if he had enough faith. The father's efforts at prayer and scripture study were immense, but his daughter's condition did not change, and he was left even more confused and bitter. This man had been the "fair-haired boy" in the eyes of his parents, and he had been able to make everything go well in his life—marriage to a beauty queen, success in business, ownership of a large house in an attractive suburban neighborhood—and he was considered a "nice, dependable guy" by all his friends. All had apparently gone well with the exception of his child's handicap.

As we were discussing his confusion about his religious faith I confronted him from a stance of affirming acceptance.

First of all your anger over the frustration presented by your daughter's handicap seems perfectly natural. Even your rageful impulses are understandable. I wonder what would happen if you could look at these impulses for what they are, without guilt and without having to act upon them. You might share them with your wife. You might also look at the areas of your life where you are too nice a guy, as you may be keeping minor irritations to yourself. They may be accumulating and focusing upon your daughter.

Secondly, let's look at why you are angry over your situation. Part of this has to do with your idea that it is unfair for you to have a handicapped child. But why shouldn't this have happened to you? Your daughter doesn't fit in with your image of yourself as the "fair-haired boy," does she? But that's your image, and you're still trying to live out your parents' expectations about you. Now, I agree that miracles do happen on occasion. But I disagree with those church folk who tell you you can make them happen with enough faith. God's the one who does miracles, and He does them when He wants to. And if He doesn't want to then He simply doesn't want to. If you really believe in God, then you must admit He must be wiser and more powerful than yourself.

Both aspects of affirming acceptance were apparent here: a recognition of the validity of his own feelings (self-acceptance) as well as affirming his life situation in spite of its painful complications. The Biblical book of Job was a useful accompanying referral for him.

I asserted a value position regarding suffering and miracles, which on the surface appears contradictory to the suggested warning, in the preceding chapter, against imposing one's philosophy upon the client. Upon closer inspection, however, we see that I was not imposing a philosophy but rather clarifying the client's own perspective—using the client's religious framework. This is an example of attitude disruption through a relabeling of the client's experience and utilizing the client's own language. The intent of the technique is to set up a homework assignment in which the client may open himself up to a new mode of experiencing a previously frustrating situation.

Another value position frequently asserted by the therapist is that of individuation, or being oneself. Being oneself involves responsible choosing and a sense of commitment or personal destiny.

A thirty-eight-year-old unmarried schoolteacher came to me

because of depression and suicidal thoughts. Soon after therapy began the depression subsided, as often occurs. Two months later it returned in a most severe fashion. She told me there was no point in her going on living. Nobody really cared about her. When she needed her friends most, like now, they pulled away from her—disliking her complaints and self-pity. If she could not be loved when she really needed it, what was the point of going on?

In the very first interview I had learned of her weekend pastime of enjoying the mountains. She was skilled at mountain climbing, hiking, snowshoeing, skiing, and river-rafting. "You're right," I said. "You can't always get people to love you when you want them to. But you know there's more to life than being loved by people. From what you told me, when you're alone in the mountains and enjoying nature you don't really need people. You are able to appreciate and make exciting use of nature in ways many people cannot. Now if you kill yourself, you'll also be doing away with that particular phase of your life. You have stated that nature is most meaningful to you. You would do away with something quite meaningful because of your bitterness over another part of your life that's frustrating. Are you being fair with yourself?"

After some further discussion about these ideas she quietly withdrew a small card from her billfold. It was a membership card to some outdoors association with a poem on the back. She read it aloud. The message of the poem was that there are times when one may feel deserted by people, but one is never deserted by nature. She was now affirming the same value position I had posed and showing that she had once understood and appreciated the same point I was now making. Suicidal depression did not again return for the duration of this woman's treatment. During the course of a year's therapy she extended her social relationships and decided upon an important shift in career as a further assertion of her own unique abilities.

This example illustrates how the therapist deals with the value of being oneself. While asserting uniqueness or individuation to be important, the therapist does not tell the person how to be himself. He must rather use what the client has already demonstrated or experienced as evidence of what can be appreciated and affirmed as a source of personal commitment. Victor Frankl elaborates upon this value stance in his description of creative, experiential, and attitudinal values.[9]

We have seen therapist-client engagement through two forms of vitalization. The first stems from the creative openness of the centering process. The second approach is used when negative reactions impede centering, so that the therapist then reveals his own negativity, often risking some degree of humiliation. The client is prepared for such therapist exposure by other forms of transparency, including sharing emotions unrelated to the client, revealing personal experiences, problem areas, and values, and the use of humor.

In spite of these efforts there will be occasions when the centering-vitalization-action process fails to occur. First of all it is unlikely that this process will occur regularly for the student therapist. He is still preoccuped with the learning of dynamics and the evaluation of goal possibilities. He is intrigued by techniques that he has not yet experienced and must undergo a trial-and-error process to discover what techniques fit his personal style best. It is not uncommon for students to declare that they were more effective therapists before they came to school, when they operated on "mere intuition." And this is an accurate perception for the most part. Education has to do with expanding knowledge and skill familiarity, and it takes time before the new becomes personally integrated and eventually intuitive.

There are also times, interestingly enough, when the centering-vitalization-action process seems to happen in spite of the therapist. It is not uncommon for a therapist to enter an interview with a sense of dread. He may be tired, bored, uncertain, confused, and not in the least excited about doing a therapy interview. Efforts at centering seem to be futile exercises. He forces himself to look interested and to listen. Yet surprisingly enough, by the end of the session he feels intimately involved with the client, vitally awake, and certain about the appropriateness of his therapeutic efforts. This is not unlike the beauty of the sunset, or the abrupt violence of an accident jolting one free of his self-preoccupations.

Inevitably, however, there will be times when even the experienced therapist is unable to move through the centering-vitalization-action process despite his efforts of personal transparency and is left with dissatisfaction and uncertainty as the interview drags on. No magic occurs. At such moments the most important move is in the direction of self-acceptance rather than blaming the client. It is perfectly OK sometimes to be personally preoccupied, confused, exhausted. The client is seeking the help of a therapist—another human being—not a God or a guru. One may or may not share his sense of ineptness. If it is troubling to the client it will probably become part of the interview content.

The centering-vitalization-action process model applies, as mentioned, not only to the direct service of psychotherapy but to the social action model as well. In the next chapter we shall see the manifestation of this model by the "absurd social activist."

Notes

1. Robert M. Pirsig, *Zen and the Art of Motorcycle Maintenance* (New York: William Morrow, 1974).

2. Harold Greenwald, "Play and Self Development," in Herbert A. Otto and John Man, eds., *Ways of Growth* (New York: The Viking Press, 1968).

3. Ram Dass, *The Only Dance There Is* (Garden City, N.Y.: Anchor Books, 1974), p. 73.

4. Joseph Chilton Pearce, *The Crack in the Cosmic Egg* (New York: Pocket Books, 1974), chapter 9.

5. Carl Rogers, "What Are You Hiding?" in Stanley Standal and Raymond Corsini, eds., *Critical Incidents in Psychotherapy* (Englewood Cliffs, N.J.: Prentice-Hall, 1959), p. 309.

6. Walter Kempler, *Principles of Gestalt Family Therapy* (Costa Mesa, Calif.: Kempler Institute, 1973).

7. Donald Krill, "Existential Psychotherapy and the Problem of Anomie," *Social Work,* vol. 14, no. 2 (April 1969): 33–49.

8. Nicolas Berdyaev, *The Destiny of Man* (New York: Harper & Brothers, 1960), pp. 84–153.

9. Viktor Frankl, *The Doctor and the Soul: From Psychotherapy to Logotherapy* (New York: Knopf, 1965), pp. 201–57.

Chapter 11

The Absurd Social Activist

In the middle of the 1960s I left the protecting walls of clinical practice and entered the vibrating halls of the university in order to pursue a new career of teaching social work practice. It was not long before my rather comfortable identity as a moderately effective social worker was deeply shaken.

It was the spring of the year, just after Martin Luther King had been assassinated, that I attended a meeting in San Francisco of the National Council on Social Welfare. I was bombarded by passionate rhetoric from conference leaders, minority caucus speakers, and students, debating and demonstrating in response to the Vietnam War, the California strike of migrant grape pickers, and the poor people's campaign in muddy Washington, D.C. There were parades in the streets, shouting of slogans, and confrontations with speakers, including the Attorney General of the United States, who was the keynote speaker for the conference.

King's death and the reactions of black leaders through the news media had left me guilty and incensed. Something must be done! I felt like a somnambulant part of the security-minded white establishment that was being attacked from several fronts: the hippies, the New Left students, the minorities, and militant social work professionals imbued with the sense that their time had come.

This same spirit of radical change continued over the next five years. At the university, the students attacked the administration, the curriculum, the faculty, and fellow students. The faculty attacked the administration at times and fought among themselves. Poverty and racism and Vietnam were focal points of change, and social workers were berating each other for their past failures in dealing with these major problems.

Those years were exciting, but also puzzling. If one found some ways to engage in radical protest, one felt some relief. Yet it never quite seemed that one was sufficiently involved, and change efforts too often seemed like some kind of predetermined scenario. Despite dramatic efforts, little seemed to change. When there was a change it appeared that new problems, equally bad, replaced the old ones. One seemed deluged with "shoulds" and "oughts" concerning one's professional mission. Yet one remained bewildered as to what to do, where to start, how far to extend oneself.

There was a sense of absurdity to the entire effort at times. Whites tried to figure out how to respond constructively to confrontations by blacks. Whatever move was made either appeared insufficient to the need or resulted in whites' being labeled racists on some new ground. If minority studies became visible in the curriculum, then efforts by whites to teach them were labeled paternalistic. When blacks and Chicanos replaced white teachers,then white faculty were accused of ignoring their responsibility to incorporate minority content in their own studies and classes. The name of the game was PROTEST, and anyone who thought he had resolved some conflict was soon aware that such change did not in the least alter the nature of the game.

Many students came into social work during those years hoping to dislodge "the establishment" in one way or another. Some of those people already departed from the profession, disappointed and cynical. Out of its own guilt, social work had fostered in its new members dreams of radical change. The dreams held promise as long as government supported innovative social-need programs (like parents financing the rebellious antics of their teenagers). But radical change, for the most part, did not occur. Social activists were fond of criticizing "clinical social workers'' for not producing significant changes in society. Yet most activists fared no better.

In our study of the intricacies of treatment we noted that some of the very ways in which helping professionals sought to be helpful could entrench old problems or create new ones, equally severe. We would find ourselves sometimes confirming people's false opinions about their own "illness and helplessness," their categorizing themselves in some rigid, oversimplistic way, their alienating themselves from their everyday life challenges and relationships by self-preoccupation, their concluding that their problems were not treatable because they seem unable to understand or make use of a therapist's particular approach, and their seeing themselves as ignorant conformers and followers of the therapist's authoritative "wisdom."

This same dilemma arises for the naïve social activist. His paternalism, authoritarianism, intellectualism (when it exists), and utopianism stem from the very passion that sends him forth on his quest for social reform. His spear is his collection of change strategies; his white steed is his righteous passion; his shield and armor consist of his avoidance of self-awareness; his band of followers are justifications for whatever he does. History is an empty word to him, his cause is the only reality.

A cycle occurs in the naïve social activist's helping efforts, which results in the impeding of change and recurring defeats. His spear is broken, little by little, with each engagement with the foe until it is rendered useless. His steed, wearied, returns home to the stable of other reassuring and complaining horses. Only his shield and armor remain solid, tarnished now by marks of cynicism and blame.

In order to understand how the naïve activist obstructs his own change efforts, I shall use the TA concept of the Karpman Triangle.[1] To this symbol have been added some descriptive terms from a Clint Eastwood Western—see Figure 11-1.

In the opening chapter we looked at a social work type called the Impulsive Helper. It was apparent that some of the attitudes

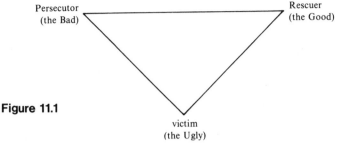

Persecutor
(the Bad)

Rescuer
(the Good)

Figure 11.1

victim
(the Ugly)

and needs of the Impulsive Helper are in us all—in fact they are motivating forces that bring most of us into the profession to begin with. One characteristic of the Impulsive Helper is his rebellion against authority in a variety of forms, at the same time holding to the secret hope that he will some day replace those "bad" authorities with his own "good, wise" paternalism. This stance results in the social worker's identifying himself (and often his profession) as "the rescuer."

The rescuer, in the Karpman triangle, requires someone to play the role of victim and someone else the role of the victim's persecutor. Victims take the forms of all social work clientele; they are found in social agencies, hospitals, clinics, jails, and state and private institutions, as well as among the minorities and the poverty-striken who have no direct relationship to any particular agency or institution. In order to quality as a victim, it is best to appear in pain as well as relatively helpless.

When clients play out this role in order to manipulate social workers, they generate their own hidden resentments for having to appear weak and helpless. Even though they allow the worker into a helping role, they despise his "helpful" paternalism. The profession has been debunked for years as a result of this dynamic.

Some workers seek to avoid this dilemma by encouraging the client group to express their own needs and frustrations—poor housing, lack of effective educational and health systems, police brutality, and so forth. Once the problems are aired and defined, the worker sees ways of helping the client group achieve their ends. This appears to be a client-centered effort as applied to a community social-action program. Too often, however, the worker maintains the rescuer-victim-persecutor perspective, which results in his "helping" the victim through an advocacy role that provokes the persecutors. Power struggle results, and if change does occur, it simply results in new problems—often worse than the previous ones.

Victims are seen as "ugly" in that they are considered weak, ignorant, powerless, brainwashed, helpless. They are often used as pawns to manipulate the system that the worker wishes to disrupt.

The persecutor's role is evil incarnate. He is a tyrannical, self-seeking, power-hungry, greedy, insensitive, bigoted, materialistic, militaristic bad guy. He cannot be dealt with in any human way. Power must be utilized as the only means of unseating him. Power tactics of any type can be easily justified on the basis of the "evil" nature of the persecutor and his "destructive" actions toward others. Insofar as social workers tend toward this model, they compound the change process. They create a new problem (the battle between good and evil) on top of the existing one. The new problem generates incredible resistance, for who wants to accept the role of being evil, wrong, and therefore having to change?

Having created victim and persecutor roles for those he deals with, the social worker is left with some of the implications of his own rescuer role. The rescuer must be good, right, wise, effective, strong, and victorious. Now the very life situations surrounding the social worker's efforts continue to challenge these very characteristics. Since it does not fit the role of a rescuer to be also ignorant, a failure, selfish, power-hungry, weak, or ineffectual, he projects those qualities onto either the victim or the persecutor. When he does this he reinforces the triangular role interplay.

There are side effects to this projection process that are self-defeating to the social worker. He often experiences disappointment with his clients and blames them for their ineffectual efforts. (Here his secret bias and prejudice become apparent to his client group.) He also blames the persecutors and so heightens the existing suspicion and antagonism which make change all the more unlikely. The worker shifts responsibility and takes on a kind of victim role himself: "If the government [persecutor] had only given us more money we could have done the job!"

This shift of responsibility reveals a key dynamic of the social worker's identity problem. Insofar as he maintains his own righteous image by blame and denial of responsibility, he tends to view his clients in the same way. Clients, too, are considered irresponsible, weak, powerless. While this nurtures the worker's view of clients as victims, it also antagonizes both clients and the public at large. These very antagonisms result in barriers to change, which in turn reinforce the social worker's sense of inadequacy. He is inclined to defend himself all the more adamantly by the very actions that continue to generate the problem. The more he blames and rescues, the more difficult it is for genuine change to occur. The social work change artist impedes change by the very nature of his effort. His guilt is compounded by his projection of blame, which in turn feeds his own sense of inadequacy and powerlessness. The more impotent his expression, the louder are his cries of complaint and the more ineffectual his efforts of influence. Empty rhetoric abounds. He moves toward either justification of violence or cynical withdrawal.

There is another way of looking at one's role as social worker in a world of distressing social problems. In this alternate position, the worker is disconnected from the Karpman triangle entirely. His stance is that of the "absurd" social activist, or worker. Instead of rescuing, he observes and responds. His social activism stems from detached observation rather than a passionate involvement. He may be assertive but is seldom angry. He experiences disappointment but is seldom guilty or resentful. When matters do not go as planned he is likely to shrug his shoulders and go in whatever direction matters went. He lives comfortably with this basic truth: "Life is what happens to you while you are planning something else."[2]

In a radio interview Ram Dass was once asked why he did not participate in a local social-political protest march. His reply was that he hoped someday to be able to do this; however he would not do so until he could experience a love for his enemy, or opposition, in such a situation. He did not wish to act in such a way as to add to the hatred already abounding in the world. When he could act out of love, his time for action would have come.

To love one's enemy is not to agree with him, but to understand him, to give him room to be whatever he is. Alan Watts pointed out that judges need lawbreakers in order to be judges. Similarly one could say that minorities need majorities in order to realize the cohesive identity and direction inherent in their minority position. Social workers need troubled people in order to be helping professionals. The action of tyranny and oppression in this world does not merely produce slavery and human suffering. It also results in creative responses to such conditions—selfless acts of loyalty, heroism, solidarity, and service to other human beings.

From a larger perspective than social workers learn in their training, a world that promotes love must necessarily promote dissension, conflict, and suffering. To eliminate the latter is also to do away with the former. Nor does such a stance lead to passive contemplation and inertia. Creative acts of loving service are inherent within the context of the world's suffering. To see oneself involved creatively and responsively in this grand play of life's forces and conditions is to be freed from much anger and resentment. One can enjoy being a helper or activist out of one's creative center as a person. Compassion, humor, and understanding replace the frustrated, overserious stance taken by so many guilt-driven rescuers.

The absurd activist comes from an inner rooting that is free from outer "matters of consequence" like Thomas Merton's *Monachos* (solitary).[3] The "solitary" character of Chapter 1 was described as the ''spontaneous strategist'' in his treatment garb (Chapter 8); now we see the combination of ''rebel'' and ''solitary'' as the ''absurd activist'' in his social-change garb.

When the rebel is opened to the perspective of the solitary, or when both rebel and solitary perspectives are combined in one person, we see a shift of viewpoint in relation to social action. Consider, for example, the rebel-solitary who is in a confrontation situation wherein he feels caught between the necessity of continued momentum and solidarity for his cause and, out of a sense of integrity, the need to exemplify the very values of his cause—honesty and fair play, for instance. Will he permit the pain of injustice to rationalize his trampling upon the human beings that are his opposition? Or will he seek understanding and compromise with both groups at the risk of losing his leadership and perhaps the cause itself? This burden of the rebel-solitary can be likened to the solitary's experience of dread. For what is the answer? How is it to be rationally determined? Reason can be used to justify either alternative. He may, at such a moment, kneel quietly alone in the dark or seek the solitude of a walk in the woods. For the rebel-solitary who is in touch with the springs of life knows that truth is not contained in any doctrine or group. It must be sought inwardly, and even when discovered it may not be free from doubt.

A certain detachment is necessary with a rebel-solitary because of the risks he must take. If he loses he may have to move on, preparing himself for another day in some other place. If he wins he is cautious with regard to any new leadership or structure that may emerge, for he knows that justice and freedom flow from the wills of men and are never inherent in any system per se.

The rebel-solitary knows a loyalty to his followers, or to the group for which he is an advocate. But he is no more inclined to take the opinions of this group as absolutes than the caseworker is to regard a client's views of the nature of his problem as literally true or what the caseworker's own theory states the client's problems, needs, goals, etc., to be. One's greatest skill as a helper is being in touch with one's own human response. One must encounter the other, or group, but encounter means one lets onself be affected by the other. One listens to the other and then to what happens within oneself, and then responds. This process continues through the entire encounter situation. One finally acts as a person bearing responsibility for his own position and not justifying it by either theory or popular opinion.

In social action, the ends sought do not automatically become absolute so as to justify any means used. The rebel-solitary can not unquestionably accept Saul A. Alinsky's "scapegoating" process as a legitimate means to fire a group of neighborhood people toward organization and increased self-power.

When possible, the means used to accomplish an action should include the same values (respect for human dignity, freedom, justice, preservation of life, or whatever) as are implicit in the ends sought. It is true that such an ethical imperative cannot be maintained in all circumstances without risk of greater wrongs through nonaction. But this means that one bears the burden of applying it wherever it can be applied in order to lessen the dehumanizing forces and activities in the world. This sensitivity to the primacy of human values is an important distinction between the rebel-solitary and other more authoritarian social-action stances.

Albert Camus described the absurd activist stance as "revolt," in contrast to revolution. "Unlike revolution," he said, "revolt can promise only a certain dignity and a relative justice." Since absolute freedom allows the strong to dominate the weak, and since absolute justice that is enforced destroys freedom within a society, the two must limit each other. For Camus the human conscience, the source of man's dignity, was his only guide in his ceaseless revolt against the ever arising evils in life. Because his revolt philosophy understood the limits of man and society and therefore spurned absolute systems that would tyrannize men, Camus saw men capable of transcending history only by his participation in the human spirit. This was an act of conscience. Yet in order to avoid a rigid and abstract moralism man would always have to derive his value-laden decisions from concrete situations.[4] Suspicion of tyranny, compassion for specific men in their circumstances, and respect for the unique transcendent quality of human personality characterized Camus's attitude.

The commitment of the absurd activist differs from that of the goal-oriented activist who is grounded in reason and the hope of shaping a "good society." Reminiscent of our earlier discussion of no-mind, the absurd worker comes from a kind of "no-model" position. Without absolutes and objective assurances about how society is supposed to function, the absurd worker seeks only a vitalized, responsive relation to social problems. His loyalty is to "the absurd" itself, which is much like Don Juan's "using death as an adviser."

All social problems are viewed in a framework of relativity. Kierkegaard's "give absolute respect to the absolute telos, and relative respect to the relative telos" applies here.[5] When viewing problems from their relative perspective, one escapes the hooks of self-importance and the necessity of controlling others to make sure things turn out "right."

For example, let us consider the activity of an absurd worker employed by the Bureau of Indian Affairs, who is studying the incidence of disease on an Indian reservation. He finds the drinking water to be contaminated because of the effects of sewage draining. Upon reporting his findings to the tribal council he is informed that the water supply is considered sacred by the tribe and that any efforts to "purify" it would be seen as contamination of its spiritual qualities. Nor would the tribe wish to disrupt its life style through the installation of a different system for handling sewage disposal. Rather than viewing disease as a given evil and the preservation of life at any cost as the given good, the absurd worker would simply point out the choices and potential consequences and risks of the issue at hand.

When there are no absolutes resulting in problems that *must* be solved, the absurd worker is left with a respect for dialogue between conflicting world views as the effort he seeks to promote. The natural outgrowth of such a stance is a pluralistic society, with no single group holding the "enlightened" answer.

If the disease of the tribe is also affecting the non-Indian population in the nearby geographical area, then the absurd worker looks to promoting the inevitable dialogical conflict.

Paul Reps describes a method of teaching problem solving that he witnessed in a small-town school in Japan. The method is called "pillow logic." Each child sits on his square cushion and presents a problem. The pillow has four sides and a middle, just as every problem does. If the left side of the pillow represents the problem, then the front side represents the opposite position. The right side represents the merging of the conflicting views of the problem, a recognition that there are "rights" and "wrongs" in relation to both sides of the problem. The rear of the pillow represents still a fourth perspective: all of this may be disregarded, it is somehow inconsequential. The four steps of problem relationships are: "wrong, 1; right, 2; both wrong and right, 3; and neither wrong nor right, 4. In conclusion, each child summarizes his presentation by cupping his hands in the middle of the pillow, affirming an unnamed center from which 1, 2, 3, 4, emerge. It is as if he holds the complete problem in his own hands at the center of the pillow."[6] He affirms all four positions.

The Westerner is quick to object that such a method leads only to navel contemplation rather than problem solving. Robert Pirsig challenges such an assumption in *Zen and the Art of Motorcycle Maintenance,* as he demonstrates that the most creative solution to a problem occurs when one gets beyond one's existing assumptions. Here we see that the absurd activist may open himself up to the "quality" of a situation, in the same manner that the therapist seeks an inner centering in relation to any given interview with a client. From this centering flows a certainty of action.

Another objection to the relativistic view of problems is that it fails to take into account the issue of social and economic power. Returning to our example of the absurd BIA worker who has posed a dialogue between the tribe and its surrounding non-Indian neighbors, it is naïve to consider such dialogue as occurring in a vacuum of human openness and interest. Whichever group possesses the most economic, social and political power may well be victorious despite "dialogical" efforts. Where will the absurd worker stand in relation to the power issue?

The roles of the community organizer have been conceptualized in four forms: the enabler, the advocate, the organizer, and the developer.[7] As with the therapist as teacher, insight-giver, model, and task-definer, specific techniques surround each defined role. We find that the absurd worker (whether therapist or social activist) seeks no particular role but instead sees himself as a strategist who may use any role that is needed. His decision for strategy stems from a view of himself as a person-engaged-in-a-situation. His creative response is his own, for which he bears complete responsibility. He does not justify his actions by outside "objective truths" and rationalizations. In one situation he may act as advocate for the less powerful group to whatever degree is necessary. In another situation he may join with the power group and seek to defuse the powder-keg situation that may erupt in violence. In still a third situation he may simply promote the confrontation and then assume an observer-enabler role for both groups. In each case he does what he must do. For Gandhi this often took the form of fasting. For Jesus it took the form of crucifixion. While to the observer these acts may appear ineffectual in the face of the problems posed, we see enormous consequences of change stemming from each action.

Both Ghandi and Jesus emphasized the importance of the personal character of the actor rather than the particular strategy employed. Appropriate strategies stem naturally from the person who has first attended to his own well being. Proper actions from an improper person will have improper results. The power that concerns the absurd worker most is personal power.

In an interview with *Psychology Today,* Carlos Castaneda related the following incident with Don Juan.

> Don Juan and I were in Tucson not long ago when they were having Earth Week. Some man was lecturing on ecology and the evils of the war in Vietnam. All the while he was smoking. Don Juan said, 'I cannot imagine he is concerned with other people's bodies when he doesn't like his own.' Our first concern should be

with ourselves. I can like my fellow man only when I am at my peak of vigor and am not depressed. To be in this condition I must keep my body trimmed. Any revolution must begin here in this body. I can alter my culture, but only from within a body that is impeccably tuned in to this weird world. For me, the real accomplishment is the art of being a warrior, which, as Don Juan says, is the only way to balance the terror of being a man with the wonder of being a man.[9]

Yasutani-roshi, a modern Zen master, related a similar view of the helping professional:

There are many people who spend all their time giving aid to the needy and joining movements for the betterment of society. To be sure, this ought not to be discounted. But their root anxiety, growing out of their false view of themselves and the universe, goes unrelieved, gnawing at their hearts and robing them of a rich, joyous life. Those who sponsor and engage in such social betterment activities look upon themselves, consciously or unconsciously, as morally superior and never bother to purge their minds of greed, anger, and delusive thinking. But the time comes when, having grown exhausted from all their restless activity, they can on longer conceal from themselves their basic anxieties about life and death. Then they seriously begin to question why life hasn't more meaning and zest. Now for the first time they wonder whether instead of trying to save others they ought not to save themselves first.[9]

The absurd worker sees no persecutor as evil incarnate. He seeks first, following Krishnamurti, to understand the source of violence within himself, realizing that he will be ineffectual in dealing with the violence of the world until he has first handled his own. Creative intelligence, Krishnamurti asserts, flows only from a mind that has become unfettered from itself.[10]

The matter of basic loyalty—to the absurd, to death as adviser, to absolute telos—involves the personal struggle toward no-mind/pragmatic-self interplay, as discussed in Chapter 5. This struggle is an enormous one, for we are part of a system that stimulates and adores ego cravings. The society we contend with in social action is also the same society we are personally co-opted by—not only in sometimes promoting its dehumanizing institutions for our own social-economic-professional security but, even more importantly, in accepting its teachings about the nature of happiness and maturity. In our very efforts to change society we commonly give expression to its philosophical under-pinnings, the seeking of personal pleasure, happiness, security, and status through ego-engendered control efforts.

The absurd worker seeks to free himself from all of this in order to function humanly as a professional. He seeks a mode of living like that of Don Juan's warrior, who "taps the world gently, stops as long as he needs to, and then swifly moves away hardly leaving a mark."[11]

There is much rhetoric these days about dignity and freedom and love and social betterment. The absurd worker knows that few people really care about such virtues beyond the rhetoric itself. He may help solve a problem, but he is not deluded into thinking he is really creating a better world. If the world im-proves, it does. If it doesn't, it doesn't. He simply acts as best he can. "Better" and "improvement" are subjective and relative value judgments of his own anyway. To be sure, we require a relative set of values in order to assess situations and give direc-tion to our professional energies. But the absurd activist also knows of another perspective that is beyond the matters of conse-quence and overserious preoccupations of his relative value sys-tem. He recalls the last outing he had on a mountain hike or a stroll by the seashore. After being moved by the profound beauty of the outing experience, he followed the trail toward home. On his way a thought popped into his head about the weighty deci-sions that awaited him in his office the next day. His response was laughter. That laughter came from a place beyond his usual matters of consequence. It was not the cynical laughter of the frustrated activist. It was rather the divine laughter that Mozart taught to Hesse's Steppenwolf. It was the laughter of the absurd activist. And at the heart of such laughter is the birth of renewed power.

Notes

1. Muriel James and Dorothy Jongeward, *Born to Win: Transactional Analysis with Gestalt Experiments* (Reading, Mass.: Addison-Wesley, 1971), p. 81.

2. Stewart W. Holmes and Chimyo Horioka, *Zen Art for Meditation* (Rutland, Vt.: Charles E. Tuttle, 1973), p. 80.

3. Thomas Merton, *Disputed Questions* (New York: Mentor-Omega, 1953), pp. 139-60.

4. John Cruickshank, *Albert Camus and the Literature of Revolt* (New York: Oxford University Press, 1960), p. 130.

5. Martin J. Heinecken, *The Moment before God* (Philadelphia: Muhlenberg Press, 1956), p. 199.

6. Paul Reps, *Square Sun, Square Moon* (Rutland, Vt.: Charles R. Tuttle, 1967), p. 19

7. Ralph M. Kramer and Harry Specht, *Readings in Community Organization Practice* (Englewood Cliffs, N.J.: Prentice-Hall, 1975), pp. 315-17.

8. Sam Keen, "Sorcerer's Apprentice," *Psychology Today,* vol. 6, no. 7 (December 1972).

9. Philip Kapleau, *The Three Pillars of Zen* (New York: Harper & Row, 1966), p. 140.

10. J. Krishnamurti, *The Awakening of Intelligence* (New York: Avon Books, 1973), pp. 374-86.

11. Carlos Castaneda, *Journey to Ixtlan: The Lessons of Don Juan* (New York: Simon & Schuster, 1972), p. 95.

Chapter 12

Directions

We have pursued the "Greening of Social Work" through varied descriptive characterizations of the existential social worker: as the solitary, the spontaneous strategist, the absurd activist. The need for a "greening" stems from the profession's own shaky image, both public and private. Social work's private, personal insecurity has displayed itself in varied ways.

The profession has sought answers from outside authorities to its own professional dilemmas. For a long time social work expected psychiatry to give answers to the multifaceted challenges of social work practice. Resenting psychiatry's failure to help (rather than seeing our own game of dumping our problems on others who know no more than we do), social work turned to the "oppressed" groups—the poor and minorities—and asked them to provide professional direction. They failed too, of course, for the expectation was ludicrous.

The public has seen through the mask of social work paternalism, recognizing its underlying insecurity as it took the forms of meddling, faulty expertise, and empty rhetoric. Other professions have also known of social work's insecurity as they have observed social workers battling among one another as well as seeing some of their envious strivings to prove themselves as good, as "professional," as other helping professionals. Social work's stance of righteousness in its efforts to scold or "awaken" other professions to social injustice has also revealed its personal insecurity.

Fortunately social work has a great deal going for it as a profession. Of all the helping professions social work has the widest array of clientele and the most varied types of problem situations challenging its concern and commitment. There is no other field of professional practice so fertile for creative and innovative efforts. The surest way to a solid identity is to accept full responsibility for one's own personal engagement with the work before one. Many social work leaders have seen this and have been telling the profession to get on with it—there is much to be done. We have talked too much already. The infighting simply diverts needed energy from the task at hand.

A second advantage for social work is that it has already experienced humiliation as a profession. Blessed are the humble-minded, for they no longer need worry about maintaining an image! Through disillusionment with oneself and others one comes to an absurdlike freedom. Having seen the ineffectiveness of psychiatry and sociology as potential guides, social work need no longer cling to the coattails of others. In recent years many social workers have been as experimental with new helping methods as have been other helping professionals. Psychiatric consultation and supervision are being replaced in many social agencies by social work expertise.

Those social workers who adhere avidly to the psychoanalytic model (and to the entire medical model, with its psychiatric authoritative structure) are becoming less and less influential in the profession. They are tending to end up in private practice in their isolated offices where they can continue to model themselves after psychiatrists. Social workers often replace psychiatrists as administrators of community mental-health centers. This is as it should be, for the present-day social worker often knows far more about community problems in relation to emotional disturbance than do psychiatrists.

As more and more social workers adopt the social-systems model of understanding problems and interventive techniques, they find themselves once again realizing the original meaning of *social* worker. An important contribution of the existential view is the realization that there is far more hope for rapid change with all kinds of clients than previously imagined. As we saw in our discussion of goal variations and the change cycle, there are far more opportunities for helping clients move toward growth than we had thought. It is not that the "unconscious" has been discarded or that the powerful reinforcement system of behaviors has been ignored. It is rather that man has again been restored to the meaning-making force that he is, and this is the source of both his strength and his dignity.

The sooner social work can free itself from its own "casework" label, the better. Associated with that term is the intrapsychic model that remains blind to man's present engagement with the forces about him. The *social* worker is coming to understand and effectively utilize the existing interaction system of significant others and their relation to wider social forces that affect them.

The rebel and the solitary both emphasize an immersion in the existing life forces of the moment. They are preoccuped neither with the past nor with intellectual abstractions. They have also freed themselves from self-identity preoccupations. Beyond pride and self-pity, they have the energy and interest to engage what is there before them. At times, they even show us how to get beyond hope—that hope which generates anger, frustration, paternalism, and cynicism. Their rooting is in the next task to be done. Their commitment is to a personal, creative response to the situation engaging them.

The unique perspective of the solitary is of particular help to modern middle-class man's sense of alienation. The solitary knows of the ambiguities, the paradoxes, and the recurring dread that characterize an anomic society. How does one deal with such dread? Who has answers? The church? The philosophers? The sociologists and psychologists? Explanations and doctrines are of little avail. The most effective answers are lived ones. It is not so important what one believes as how one lives. It is his creativity or his passion, his humility or his kindness, his courage or his sense of beauty and joy, that reveal his answers to the questions of dread and nothingness.

We can learn from the solitary that it is not necessary to be a genius, a prophet, or a saint in order to respond to the lost, alienated client. But it is important to be the lived answer to the questions of dread that one essentially is as a person. One's lived answer may take one of the forms described in Chapter 1 as ways of encountering dread. One's lived answer may also be simply an honest confusion of doubt and the lack of any answer. On the other hand, one's answer may take the form of offering some very specific values, as discussed in Chapter 10.

The solitary asserts that we must first be able to recognize the effects of anomie or alienation upon our clients and upon ourselves. Then we must be willing to deal with this aspect of the problem, when appropriate, by revealing our own responses (and the responses of others) to the same condition that plagues the client. We are not presenting an answer here but the various directions in which people (including ourselves) have moved in their efforts to find a personally satisfying solution. We are exposing our own humanity in sharing a condition as an equal with our client. We help people face the terror of existence rather than flee from it with negative self-judgments or by demanding that others around them change.

Basic to a profession's efforts to rejuvenate itself are its uses of research and education. Existentialism and Zen have sometimes been discredited as being antiscientific because of their emphasis upon subjectivity and the irrational. Paradoxically, the existential person is often more capable of the type of detachment required by the scientific method than are many of his social work brothers. When one is freed from the hope of proving a position through one's research, one can look honestly at the outcome with less distortion or anxiety. What has made research in social science so often suspect is the undergirding assumptions made by researchers to justify their position. We have seen abuses of research in the efforts of psychotherapists to sell their new methods. We have seen incredibly complex and expensive programs for social improvement undertaken with either minimal or otherwise prejudicial research that is intended to justify further funding. Research is too often used as a political tool to maintain power, which is blasphemy to the scientific method.

The researcher who holds to the integrity of scientific exploration seeks simply to explore and observe and report what is there. Robert Powell likens this stance to the Zen way of seeing life as it is, without distorting hopes, attachments, or fears. He also clarifies the boundaries of the scientific method:

> It must be clear... that the scientist is simply seeking a new hypothesis which fits the observed phenomena better than did a previous one; but this is still within the sphere of "models" of the universe, of reality—and that is all he is concerned with. Therefore, he is *not* seeking Truth, for if he were he would at once give up the effort to "reconstruct" reality by means of models and mathematical equations which at best can only have the same relation to Reality as a photographic image has to its original (it lacks a full dimension!). In other words the scientist lives in a world of abstractions; he is only concerned with "making things work" by systematized common sense. Basically he is a "concept merchant" for the concepts that give him the results he is seeking.[1]

On the other hand the existential social worker, acting as strategist, is able to use research as a tool for effecting change without doing violence to the research method itself. It is not always the outcome of research that produces change but the very process of research engagement itself.

On three occasions I was involved with mental health centers with staff morale problems. In each case one aspect of the low morale had to do with the apparent need for community outreach. Each clinic, despite its "community commitment," was busying itself with the clinical problems of clients who came knocking at its doors. The staff in administrative control were comfortable in their use of authoritative expertise with other staff when maintaining this "clinical" focus. The frustrated staff members were not merely wanting to try something new. They were responding to needs of the community that they had heard about from school principals, welfare workers, nurses, police, judges, or ministers. Many of the most troublesome family and social problems were occurring with people who had no interest in seeking help at a mental health clinic.

When these issues were discussed at staff meetings they could be easily dismissed by the staff in power. Such problems were relegated to the category of "untreatable" or else exaggerations by disgruntled community "front-line professionals." The community commitment was being "satisfactorily handled" by periodic case consultants with various groups of these front-line helping professionals.

In each instance, change of clinic attitude began to occur when concerned staff proposed research efforts. Since research (like God, mother, and country) was considered a reasonable approach to any problem, it was permitted. The research varied in form. In one instance it involved a survey of the attitudes and opinions of all referring front-line helping professionals. In another, the survey was of staff attitudes about the existing service activity of the clinic: the use of manpower time and the nature of results achieved. A third study sought data from schools, welfare departments, and probation officers as to the geographical areas in the community most heavily populated with serious problem cases.

The very effort to look at further data engaged staff members with the issue of change in a new way, which in turn generated mounting interest, excitement, and motivation for pursuing the issue with more vigor. As morale improved, so did the sense of concerned unity among staff members. The resulting pressure was too much for the administrative staff to contain, and changes began to occur. It was not the outcome of research that provided the impetus for movement in these three examples but the activity of the research effort itself.

The existential model suggests the need for research in relation to some of the assumptions and directions posed. Is it accurate to say that an eclectic model of treatment is more effective with clients than the use of a single theory-skill position that is carefully understood and wisely used by a therapist? The assumption to be examined is that clients are responsive to different techniques and that no single therapeutic system incorporates a wide enough array of potential techniques to serve adequately the variety of needs among clients.

A common activity among agencies that should be carefully studied is the way clients are assigned for therapy. Even when an agency includes staff of varying skill areas, how are clients assigned to therapists? In many cases agencies make assignments more on the basis of openings by therapists than on the basis of the need of the client. Varied forms of individual therapy, group therapy, or family therapy are used more as a result of the happenstance timing of a client's appearance for help than of a careful understanding of what mode and techniques of therapy will best fit his needs. This haphazard use of varied therapy approaches is not responsible eclectic therapy.

A second area needing research exploration has to do with the understanding of pathology as well as the conception of change characteristic of varied therapeutic systems. It is the contention of the existential social worker that therapies stressing the intrapsychic model, in contrast to the interpersonal (S-O-S) model, may actually encourage alienation on the part of the clients and, similarly, that rational self-understanding as the major tool used to produce change, in contrast to the experiential-interpersonal approaches that utilize more short-term, task-oriented, problem-engagement techniques, will also encourage alienation from self and others. These assumptions need further clarification through research into therapy methods and results.

A third assumption suggested by the existential model has to do with our understanding of and work with psychotics and psychopaths. The assumption is that in certain respects these people are more honestly in touch with the realities of the human condition than are most others with personality disorders, neurotic symptoms, and even many people considered free of emotional symptomatology. This issue raises questions as to the nature of the unconscious, of the forces at work in primary process. The difficulty in researching such areas is in finding a nonbiased researcher to do the work and interpret the findings. There is the added difficulty of getting the professional community to take the results of such research seriously when they reveal unexpected conclusions. For example, the results of research on psychic phenomena at Duke University have been largely ignored by the psychology profession. Even when accepted, they tend to be relegated to the categories of "interesting" and "amusing" rather than as having important implications for our existing theories of personality.

Existential thought has already made an impact on higher education through the writing of Carl Rogers and George Kneller.[2] Krishnamurti and Martin Buber both have related their philosophical perspectives to education. Don Juan himself demonstrates an existential teaching-learning model. Social work education has long needed such contributions. Just as social workers have tended to see their clients as weaker, than they are, in order to justify their own paternalistic efforts, so too have teachers of social work imagined their students to be more ignorant or more immature than is usually the case. Social work education has come from an era of pedantic "spoonfeeding" of students, encouraged by teachers' adherence to a theory of knowledge taken as unquestionably true. What was labeled "good, basic casework" was this single, limited perspective on understanding pathology and treatment. The rigidities had been so strong that the differences between Rankian and Freudian approaches in social work could be resolved only by declaring the existence of two different "schools" of social work; the functional and the dynamic.

It is no wonder that the paternalistic model has dominated social work for so many years. Students used the same model with clients that was being used on them by supervisors and classroom teachers. Faculty even made "educational diagnoses" of students. Just as with clients, such diagnostic assessments were used to rationalize authoritative decision-making about the students' "needs, readiness, talents, and prognosis." Today, with theoretical underpinnings being challenged and practice opportunities much more varied and experimental, schools of social work have moved in the direction of student-centered rather than theory-centered education. This change also has been a response to student protests of the 1960s. Compatible with existential client-centered treatment, student-centered teaching places responsibility for learning squarely with the student. The teacher is no longer protective of the students' "fragile" egos. The student must discover himself in relation to his own personal integration of practice, theory, philosophy, and subjective awareness. The very breadth of social work's fields of practice permits students to explore a wide variety of knowledge and talent.

Related to student-centered teaching is the increasing emphasis upon experiential learning, in contrast to intellectual-content understanding. The personal, artistic components of social work are at last being spotlighted. The use of role plays, of sound and video tapes, and encounter and gestalt experiences bring students more intimately in contact with one another as well as making them more sharply aware of themselves.

Growth through direct engagement with experience has been the thrust of existential thinking. Choice, responsibility, and heightened self-awareness occur primarily through action, not intellectualizing. Earlier efforts of social work faculty to shield students from painful experiences impeded learning. Not only were students being taught to view themselves as irresponsible victims, like their clients, but they tended to see both themselves and their clients as more fragile than they were. Many students could hardly wait to get themselves analyzed. Self-awareness and growth were expected to come in that protected package of analyst and couch. Without such in-depth analysis a student could hardly hope to trust his own emotions and intuitions, and he would naturally be ineffective with his clients. So personal confidence was undermined in students in relation to their own growth potential.

Many agencies with training programs have been more daring and effective in clinical teaching than have been schools of social work. By using two-way screens and video tapes for all student interviews, they not only examine but actually capture for replay the life process of a student-client interaction system. How clearly superior this is to process recordings written by students for their supervisors after the fact of the interview itself!

Ideally, not only should the experiential emphasis in teaching use the direct-exposure approach described above, but also field experience and classroom should be intertwined. Faculty teaching in classrooms should also be doing some supervision and having a very clear understanding of the clients with whom students are working. Faculty members should expose themselves through videotape, role plays, and two-way screens if they expect students to do this. The social work school of the future should incorporate direct-treatment programs within its walls, as do most training programs in psychology and psychiatry. The same field-class integrative model should be used for community-organization projects. The actual location of schools of social work has tended to protect faculty from some of the hard realities of direct practice. There is no reason why all buildings need be on campus. To have part of the school in the heart of a poor ghetto neighborhood, acting as community center as well as graduate school, would provide a variety of opportunities for direct-exposure learning in relation to group work and community-action efforts.

The "greening" of social work implies the spread of influence of a particular philosophy and life style. This can occur if social work heeds the messages of the rebels and solitaries already in its ranks. But, perhaps more important, schools of social work must find ways of discovering budding rebels and solitaries among students and encouraging their professional development along the philosophical lines that are their natural calling.

Many students today are potential rebels or solitaries as a result of their varied experiences with social action, protest, encounter groups, mind-expanding drugs, meditation, communal living, and mysticism. Not that these experiences are in any sense prerequisites, but they do lend validity to a life perspective rooted in personal feeling- and intuition-laden experiences in contrast to the objectified, systematized, categorized approaches that have dominated most social work professional training to date. The rebel and the solitary as social work professionals are more, however, than feeling-oriented people. The candor, compassion, and detachment that characterize them stem from a discipline and sensitivity developed through considerable experience. Students need examples from the professionals who have, or at least understand, the rebel and solitary perspectives.

Like the man fearful of his shadow and his footsteps, perhaps the social work profession has been running too fast. It has been plagued by its own guilt and thus is a too ready respondent to the spurs of the impulsive helpers and the ɔlutions of the rational organizers. The profession must again learn patience. It must be able to find some comfort with ambiguity. Let it be more attuned to the voices of the rebel and solitary—not only in others, but within each of us.

Notes

1. Robert Powell, *Zen and Reality* (New York: Viking Press, 1961), p. 123.
2. Carl Rogers, *Freedom to Learn* (Columbus: Charles S. Merrill, 1969); George F. Kneller, *Existentialism and Education* (New York: John Wiley & Sons, 1958).

Bibliography

ALLPORT, GORDON. *Letters from Jenny*. New York: Harcourt, Brace & World, 1965.

ANGYAL, ANDRAS. *Neurosis and Treatment*. New York: John Wiley & Sons, 1965.

BANDLER, RICHARD, and JOHN GRINDER. *The Structure of Magic*. Palo Alto, Calif.: Science and Behavior Books, 1975.

BARNES, HAZEL. *The Literature of Possibility: A Study of Humanistic Existentialism*. Lincoln: University of Nebraska Press, 1959.

BARRETT, WILLIAM. *Irrational Man*. Garden City, N.Y.: Doubleday, 1958.

BERDYAEV, NIKOLAI. *Slavery and Freedom*. New York: Charles Scribners, 1944.

BINSWANGER, LUDWIG. *Being in the World*. New York: Basic Books, 1963.

BOROWITZ, EUGENE. *A Layman's Guide to Religious Existentialism*. New York: Delta, 1966.

BOSS, MEDARD. *Psychoanalysis and Daseinsanalysis*. New York: Basic Books, 1963.

BRADFORD, KIRK A. *Existentialism and Casework*. Jericho, N.Y.: Exposition Press, 1969.

BUBER, MARTIN. *Between Man and Man*. Boston: Beacom Press, 1955.

———. *The Knowledge of Man*. New York: Harper & Row, 1965.

BURTON, ARTHUR, ed. *Encounter*. San Francisco: Jossey-Bass, 1969.

CAMUS, ALBERT. *The Rebel*. New York: Alfred A. Knopf, 1969.

CASTANEDA, CARLOS. *Tales of Power*. New York: Simon & Schuster, 1974.

―――. *Journey to Ixtlan*. New York: Simon & Schuster, 1972.

CURRY, ANDREW. "Toward a Phenomenological Study of the Family," *Existential Psychiatry*, 6, no. 27 (Spring 1967): 35–44.

DE MILLE, RICHARD. *Castaneda's Journey: The Power and the Allegory*. Santa Barbara, Calif.: Capra Press, 1976.

DURKIN, HELEN. *The Group in Depth*. New York: International Universities Press, 1964.

ELLIS, ALBERT. *Humanistic Psychotherapy: The Rational-Emotive Approach*. New York: McGraw-Hill, 1974.

FARBER, LESLIE. *The Ways of the Will*. New York: Harper Colophon Books, 1966.

FRANK FARRELLY. *Provocative Therapy*. Madison: Family, Social, Psychotherapy Service, 1974.

FORD, DONALD, and HUGH URBAN. *Systems of Psychotherapy*. New York: John Wiley & Sons, 1964, Chapter 12.

FRANKL, VIKTOR E. *The Doctor and the Soul: From Psychotherapy to Logotherapy*. New York: Alfred A. Knopf, 1965.

―――. *Man's Search for Meaning: An Introduction to Logotherapy*. Boston: Beacon Press, 1962.

―――. *Psychotherapy and Existentialism: Selected Papers on Logotherapy*. New York: Simon & Schuster, 1967.

FRONHBERG, MARGERY. "Existentialism: An Introduction to the Contemporary Conscience," *Perceptions*, 1, no. 1 (School of Social Work, San Diego State College, Spring 1967): 24–32.

GLASSER, WILLIAM. *Reality Therapy*. New York: Harper & Row, 1965.

GYARFAS, MARY. "Social Science, Technology and Social Work: A Caseworker's View," *Social Service Review*, 43, no. 3 (September 1969): 259–273.

HALEY, JAY. *Problem Solving Therapy*. San Francisco: Jossey-Bass, 1976.

―――. *Strategies of Psychotherapy*. New York: Grune & Stratton, 1963.

HEINECKEN, MARTIN J. *The Moment Before God*. Philadelphia: Muhlenberg Press, 1956. A study on the thought of Kierkegaard.

IMRE, ROBERTA WELLS. "A Theological View of Social Casework," *Social Casework,* 52, no. 9 (November 1971): 578–585.

JOURARD, SYDNEY. *The Transparent Self.* Princeton, N.J.: Van Nostrand, 1964.

JUNG, C. G. *Modern Man in Search of a Soul.* New York: Harcourt, Brace, 1933.

KATZ, ROBERT L. *Empathy.* New York: Free Press, 1963.

KEMPLER, WALTER. *Principles of Gestalt Family Therapy.* Costa Mesa, Calif.: Kempler Institute, 1973.

KLEIN, ALAN F. *Social Work Through Group Process.* Albany, N.Y.: School of Social Welfare, State University of New York, 1970.

KRILL, DONALD F. "Existentialism: A Philosophy for Our Current Revolutions," *The Social Service Review,* 40, no. 3 (September 1966): 289–301.

———. "Existential Psychotherapy and the Problem of Anomie," *Social Work,* 14, no. 2 (April 1969): 33–49

———. "Psychoanalysis, Mowrer and the Existentialists," *Pastoral Psychology,* 16 (October 1965): 27–36.

———. "A Framework for Determining Client Modifiability," *Social Casework.* 49, no. 10 (December 1968): 602–611.

KRISHNAMURTI, J. *The Flight of the Eagle.* New York: Harper & Row, 1971.

KUCKLEMANS, JOSEPH J. *Phenomenology: The Philosophy of Edmund Husserl and Its Interpretation.* Garden City, N.Y.: Doubleday, 1967.

LAING, R. D. *The Politics of Experience.* Baltimore: Penguin, 1967.

———. *The Divided Self.* Baltimore: Penguin, 1964.

MASLOW, ABRAHAM H. *Towardia Psychology of Being.* Princeton, N.J.: Van Nostrand, 1962.

MAY, ROLLO. *Psychology and the Human Dilemma.* Princeton, N.J.: Van Nostrand, 1967.

———, ed. *Existential Psychology.* New York: Random House, 1961.

MAY, ROLLO, ANGEL ELLENBERGER, and H. F. ELLENBERGER, eds. *Existence: A New Dimension in Psychiatry and Psychology.* New York: Basic Books, 1958.

MERTON, THOMAS. *Disputed Questions.* New York: Mentor-Omega, 1953.

MOUSTAKAS, CLARK, ed. *The Self: Explorations in Personal Growth.* New York: Harper & Row, 1956.

MOWRER, O. HOBART. *The Crisis in Psychiatry and Religion.* Princeton, N.J.: Van Nostrand, 1961.

NUTTIN, JOSEPH. *Psychoanalysis and Personality.* New York: Mentor-Omega, 1962.

ORNSTEIN, ROBERT E. *The Psychology of Consciousness.* Columbus, O.: W. H. Freeman, 1971.

PEARCE, JOSEPH CHILTON. *Exploring the Crack in the Cosmic Egg.* New York: Julian Press, 1974. Paperback, New York: Pocket Books, 1975.

—————. *The Crack in the Cosmic Egg.* New York: Julian Press, 1971. Paperback, New York: Pocket Books, 1974.

PERLS, FREDERICK S. *Gestalt Therapy Verbatim.* Lafayette, Calif.: Real People Press, 1969.

PIRSIG, ROBERT. *Zen and the Art of Motorcycle Maintenance.* New York: Bantam, 1975.

REICH, CHARLES. *The Greening of America.* New York: Random House, 1970.

REINHARDT, KURT F. *The Existentialist Revolt.* New York: Frederick Ungar, 1952.

ROBINSON, JOHN A. T. *Exploration into God.* Stanford, Calif.: Stanford University Press, 1964.

ROGERS, CARL. *On Becoming a Person.* Boston: Houghton Mifflin, 1961.

RUBIN, GERALD K. "Helping A Clinic Patient Modify Self-destructive Thinking," *Social Work,* 7, no. 1 (January 1962): 76–80.

RUBINOFF, LIONEL. *The Pornography of Power.* New York: Ballantine, 1969.

SALOMON, ELIZABETH. "Humanistic Values and Social Casework," *Social Casework,* 48 (January 1967): 26–32.

SATIR, VIRGINIA. *Conjoint Family Therapy.* Palo Alto, Calif.: Science and Behavior Books, 1964.

SINSHEIMER, ROBERT. "The Existential Casework Relationship," *Social Casework,* 50, no. 2 (February 1969): 67–73.

SKINNER, B. F. *Beyond Freedom and Dignity*. New York: Alfred A. Knopf, 1971.

STRETCH, JOHN. "Existentialism: A Proposed Philosophical Orientation for Social Work," *Social Work,* 12, no. 4 (October 1967): 97–102.

SUTHERLAND, RICHARD. "Choosing as Therapeutic Aim, Method and Philosophy," *Journal of Existential Psychiatry,* 2, no. 8 (Spring 1962): 371–392.

TAFT, J. "A Conception of the Growth Underlying Social Casework Practice," *Social Casework,* 21. (1950): 311–316.

TEILHARD DE CHARDIN, PIERRE. *The Phenomenon of Man*. New York: Harper & Row, 1959.

TIRYAKIAN, EDWARD A. *Sociologism and Existentialism*. Englewood Cliffs, N.J.: Prentice-Hall, 1962.

TILLICH, PAUL. *The Courage to Be*. New Haven: Yale University Press, 1952.

———. *Love, Power and Justice*. New York: Oxford University Press, 1960.

VATAI LASZLO. *Man and His Tragic Life*. New York: Philosophical Library, 1954.

WATTS, ALAN. *The Book*. New York: Collier Books, 1967.

WATZLAWICK, PAUL, JOHN WEAKLAND, and RICHARD FISCH. *Change: Principles of Problem Formation and Problem Resolution*. New York: W. W. Norton, 1974.

WATZLAWICK, PAUL. *How Real Is Real?* New York: Random House, 1967.

WEISS, DAVID. *Existential Human Relations*. Montreal: Dawson College Press, 1975.

———. "The Ontological Dimension—Social Casework," *The Social Worker* (CASW, June 1962).

———. "The Existential Approach to Social Work," *Viewpoints* (Montreal, Spring 1976).

———. "Social Work as Authentication," *The Social Worker* (CASW, February 1968).

———. "Self Determination in Social Work: An Existential Dialogue," *The Social Worker* (CASW November 1969).

————. "Social Work as Encountering," *Journal of Jewish Communal Service,* Spring, 1970.

————. "Social Work as Healing and Revealing," *Intervention,* no. 50 (Summer 1970).

————. "The Existential Approach to Fields of Practice," *Intervention,* no. 55 (Fall 1971).

————. "The Living Language of Encountering: Homage to Martin Buber 1878–1965," *Intervention,* no. 57 (Spring, 1972).

WHEELIS, ALLEN. *The Quest for Identity.* New York: W. W. Norton, 1958.

WINTHROP, HENRY. "Culture, Mass Society, and the American Metropolis: High Culture and Middlebrow Culture: An Existential View," *Journal of Existentialism,* 8, no. 27 (Spring 1967): 371.

Index